DAY TRADING FOR BEGINNERS

HOW TO TRADE AND MAKE MONEY WITH DAY STRATEGY THROUGH A BEGINNER GUIDE TO LEARN THE BEST STRATEGIES FOR CREATING YOUR PASSIVE INCOME FOR A LIVING. INCLUDES TIPS AND TRICKS

MATTHEW SWING

TABLE OF CONTENTS

Introduction

The in-depth understanding of day trading cannot be achieved only from its mere definition. There is still more that encompasses day trading that you would require to know and understand before regarding yourself as an expert in day trading. Especially for you as a beginner, the journey is still long, but with a clear mindset and focus, you will soon get to understand all that revolves around day trading and be fully proficient. With day trading, it is absolutely possible to earn good pay for very few hours within a day. However, individuals who get into the market without a clear understanding of day trading always end up getting enormous losses.

Having a strategy, you realize that for all the various methods of carrying out any trade, require a certain strategy. You ought to adopt or rather create one that best suits you. Failure to which you risk making huge losses in your trade. Day trading is not just like any other kind of trade, which you would just succeed in a whim without a clear strategy. You need to ask yourself various questions like how will you get into the trade, what do you need to have to get into the trade, or how much in terms of profits do you think you will get?, how many shares of stock would you purchase with the money that you have set aside for the day trade, how much would you stand to lose in case things go haywire? Having these questions in mind, they will act as driving forces towards the know-how of starting the trade. Implementing them once you are in the trade gives you a kind of a method that you can try out over and over, analyze your results, and find out whether it works in your favor. You can also develop a strategy from other people as well who have been in the trade and have tried it and have worked for them.

To be successful in day trade, you will require to do as much practice as possible, especially before you decide on using your own hard-earned money in the trade. As the old saying goes, "practice makes perfect". You do not necessarily have to have high educational qualifications to make it in day trading. Practice hard to find that one strategy that suits you. The practice here is using demo accounts. Here you are at liberty to try out even your most recently learned strategy and see whether it works out well for you. When you find yourself being profitable in a demo account, then from there, you can decide to get into real trading. Use the same strategy that you have been using in your demo account. The idea here of practicing as much as possible is to spot repeating patterns. However, the demo account, to some extent, may not be similar to real trading in terms of the pressures and associated risks, but it still plays a critical role in ensuring that you acquire the necessary confidence and understand better your best trading method. Due to this, at first, you may realize that your trade may fail to do well as it was when you were doing the demo. This should not worry you. It is so natural and is expected. The choice of the demo account would, to some extent, also matter considering that some do not expire; hence, they provide you with an opportunity to trade as much as you would wish to.

The issue of the amount of capital that you would require to get into the trade is also a key factor. This determines how much you get as returns in case of profits within a day of trading. The minimum amount to start with maybe specific with some markets, while others do not have a set minimum. The majority of the traders, on the other hand, only put in the capital that they can afford to lose. Somehow this helps eliminate emotions while in the trade hence enable them to make sound decisions. Moreover, having very low capital for you day trade may disadvantage you as you may end up paying extremely high commissions while at the same time receive poor order executions? You will realize that all markets usually offer good profit potential. Hence the only factor that stands out is the amount of capital you invest — putting these into consideration, having a large capital to trade with stands out as an added advantage in Day Trading. Nonetheless, do not be misguided into believing that day trading is one quick, easy way of making money overnight. This only applies when you are well aware of the trade; have defined clear strategies and a deep understanding of your market. Moreover, despite the many skills, luck in one way or another, as well as good timing skills, counts.

You also need to understand that for day trade, you will require to have a broker. Your choice of a broker is quite critical, as this is the person whom you in one way or the other trust with all of your capital. Here you may decide to settle with the online broker whom you opened the demo account with or choose another. The majority of the day traders usually prefer those brokers who base their charges per share instead of per trade. In the case where a broker charges high commissions, then he can negatively affect your profitability based on your day's strategy despite you wanting to save your profits by looking for low fee brokers. You have to ensure that they are quite reliable; otherwise, you may end up losing a lot of your dollars. It would also be advisable to seek the services of those brokers who provide you with the opportunity to place multiple orders.

You also need to know when it is that you should be carrying out your trade. The consistency in this not only works for the beginners but the pros as well. You will not have to spend the whole day trading necessarily. The best way to achieve this consistency is to trade for say two to three hours. Understanding the best time to focus on doing your trades based on market volatility is also of the essence. Try knowing when the price moves are quite sizable and offer the best profit potential.

It would be wise to understand how to manage your risks. This involves the day's risks as well as the trading risks. For trade risks, you can reduce them to as much as 1% for each trade. This can be achieved by setting a stop loss. This will remove you from the trade, in case you start losing significantly against you. For the day's risk, you understand that one single day has the capability to ruin your entire week or even month! Setting it at around 3% of your entire capital is quite manageable. This protects you from being emotional as you make decisions in the trade as well; no matter how strong you may think you are when faced with enormous losses, your psychology always starts making hopeless and fruitless decisions that end up ruining your trade completely. Being affected emotionally by your trade is a clear indication that you are trading too much money. Day trading is more of betting, making bets in a way that the probability of winning is to your advantage, then is your ultimate success in day trade. However, the magnitude of the percentage loss that you decide on taking can change depending on the number of wins that you get as compared to the losses.

Chapter 1 Why Learning Day Trading Today Is An Opportunity?

T his begs the question, why learning day trading today is an opportunity? There are many advantages of day trading so let's take the time to look at some of them.

Higher ROI on Time Investment

ROI stands for return on investment and in this case, I'm referring to the amount of time you need to spend trading in order to achieve a good return on your money. Day traders do not hold positions (an active trade is called a position) for more than the length of the market session.

This means that you open a trade in the morning and exit by the time the market closes. The rest of the day is open for you! In America, the market is open from 9A.M to 5 P.M. This sounds like holding a 9 to 5 job but to be honest, there are many variations. Some traders trade just the morning session while some trade just the post lunch session.

Trading volumes ebb and flow throughout the day and you may find that your most profitable trades occur in the three hour window in the morning before the lunch session begins at 12 P.M. Good day traders can earn returns of over 50% on their money after commissions so for a three hour workday, this is a pretty good payment!

Zero Gap Risk

Most beginners don't take this into account but gaps are one of the biggest reasons traders lose money. So what is a gap? Let's say the market closes at level X on Monday. It is now closed and will reopen on Tuesday morning. In the intervening time, despite there being no orders being transacted, supply and demand for stocks doesn't stop.

The effects of these afterhours supply and demand will manifest in the opening price on Tuesday. It might open at (X+1) or at (X-50.) The difference in the previous closing price and the next opening price is called a gap. In the FX market, volatility is so high that gaps occur within a market session.

The FX market runs for 24 hours and closes only on the weekend. This means that the nature of order flow changes throughout the day. What happened in the Asian session, when Japan and Australia are online, can be very different from when London and Europe comes online and even more different from when New York comes online. Thus, you will see gaps form during the day, despite the market always being open.

With day trading in stocks, you'll close your position at the end of the day and will see zero gap risk. In FX, you can close your position as a session ends and this will reduce your risk significantly as well.

Faster Feedback

Most beginners stay away from day trading because they feel that the market moves too fast. This is true. You'll be trading lower time frames and as a result, you'll find that prices will change on a much quicker basis. Every five minutes or so, you'll have to reevaluate your stance in the market and will need to make decisions.

This fast pace of trading is not for everyone. The flip side is that if you're learning to trade, you'll gain feedback a lot faster and will improve at a faster rate. The faster you incorporate market feedback into your trading, the sooner you'll become successful. Instead of waiting for weeks or months to see if your trade works out, you'll know within a few minutes if you're doing things correctly.

Chapter 2 What Is Day Trading And How To Get Started?

What is day trading?

The stock market is a vast place and there are millions of trades that take place all over the world, within a single day. There are both buyers and sellers in the market and they will all have the same motive in mind; to increase their wealth potential.

Of all these trades, not everything will be of the same nature. Some will be long-term investments and some short. Long-term investments refer to those that are held for a long period of time. They are preferred by those who are not in a hurry to make money. Short-term investments on the other hand are those that are liquidated within a short period of time. They are not meant to be held for a long time, as the owners will be interested in disposing them off early.

Short-term investments can be of many types based on the time that they are held. Some can be held for a month, some for a week and some will be disposed off on the same day.

Better known as Intraday trading, day trading is one of the most preferred ways to trade in the stock market. Preferred mostly by those willing to part with their investment within a single day and realize a profit, or loss, from.

Intraday traders are interested in realizing a profit by capitalizing on the difference in the rates of these securities as opposed to long-term investors who will be in it for the Dividends.

Difference in opinions

There is a difference of opinion in the investing community on what exactly day trading is. Some believe that the shares have to be bought and sold on the same day in order for it to count as intraday trading. Others are of the opinion that people holding it for 5 days will also count for intraday trading. When you buy a stock, you don't have to pay for it for 5 days and will also have a grace period of 2 extra days. And if you dispose of your stock within that time then it will count as intraday trading.

Whatever the case, intraday trading is a great choice for both beginners and old hands. There are tips and tricks for you to follow to reel in the best results through your intraday investments. Before we proceed to understanding each type, let us look at how you can get started with intraday trading.

Laptop

The very first thing to buy is a laptop for yourself. You have to dedicate an entire computer system to day trading, as you will have to keep an eye on the markets the whole time. If you are using the computer for some other purpose as well then you might end up missing a good deal. You have to set up a different workstation if possible and only then will you be able to take it up seriously. It is a good idea to invest in a desktop as that will help you stay put in one place instead of carrying your computer around. You can also set up a computer system. Start by picking a good spot at home where you can set up the computer system. It is best for you to pick a desktop system as opposed to a laptop as the desktop will help you stay put in a single place. You will also have to have a high-speed Internet connection, without which you will not be able to buy and sell stocks fast enough.

Internet

The next thing is to get a good Internet connection. As you know, intraday trading requires you to look at the prices of stocks on a minute-to-minute basis and that is only possible if you have a fast and reliable Internet connection. You have to have a back-up system in place as well to remain prepared for any erratic Internet. You must also have a connection on your phone, which will help you access the Internet from anywhere and keep an eye on the different stock prices.

Account

The next step is to open a trading account with a company. The trading company should be well reputed and should help you trade comfortably. You will not have to go through a lengthy process to open one and if your banker provides the service then you can ask them to open up the account for you. Remember that you need an online account in particular so that you can trade by yourself. Next, you have to create a trading account. It is what you will be using to buy and sell your stocks. The trading account should be opened through a brokering firm who will act as a connection between you and the stock market. You have to pick a firm that is well reputed in order to have a pleasant work experience. Read up some reviews about them before deciding upon the company. The account is simple to open and operate. They will ask you for some key information about yourself, after which they will issue you an online login and password.

Software

The next step is to have the software installed. The software here refers to the one that you will be using for your intraday trading. The trading company that you sign up with will provide you with the software and will also send across personnel to install it on your computer. If it is freely available on the Internet, then you can download it yourself. Once done, you will have to create a login account and only then can you start using it.

Broker

The next step is to employ a broker. A broker is one who helps you buy and sell the shares. But you have a choice. If you are willing to do it by yourself then you can employ a part time broker or not employ one at all. If you don't have the time for it and need help then you can employ a full time broker who will do everything for you including researching, buying, selling etc. The former will charge you quite less for his service whereas the latter will charge you much more. Remember that you have to employ an intraday broker in particular, as they will have knowledge on how to conduct the trading activities in the intraday market. Brokers can be quite an important part of your investment strategy, as they will have access to all the important information about your stocks. You have to find a broker that is well experienced and can help you pick the right stocks. Before you hire a broker, ensure that you do a thorough background check to see if they are good candidates for you.

Knowledge

The next step is for you to equip yourself with the knowledge of carrying out day-to-day trades in the intraday market. You have to go through other information that is present online and equip yourself as much as possible with the right type of information and trade with ease.

Research

You have to do a small research on the market trends before investing. That will help you invest in the right places. You have to look at the best stocks to invest in, in the individual categories. Once you do your research, make a list of the 5 best companies to invest with in the different categories and then further narrow them down.

Budget

It is important for you to set yourself a budget if you wish to trade wisely. The budget should be such that it allows you to invest in a variety of stocks and still remain with spare money that you can divert towards a backup account. The budget should be based on your spending capacity and how much you have at your disposal. It is best to consult an expert first to know how much you must ideally hold.

Buy stocks

Next, you have to buy the stocks. These stocks are picked from the stock market and you have to have a good variety to start with. It is best to observe the stocks for some time before making your final decision. Once you have made your choice, you can buy the stocks.

Generate a Watch list

A watch list can come in handy when you wish to keep track of the different stocks you own. A watch list is meant to help you study the different stocks so that you know exactly when to sell them. If you think a particular stock is going the way you want it to, then you can generate another list with just that one stock in it.

Sell your stocks

The next logical step is for you to sell your stocks. You have to ring in a profit and the only way to do so is by selling whatever is in your possession. But you have to ensure that you sell it when the stock's price is high. Don't sell it just to get rid of it, you have to remain patient and sell it only when the right time comes.

Repeat the steps

The next step is for you to repeat all the above steps, again. So, start by buying stocks, hold them and then sell them. You have to do this on a daily basis if you plan on being an intraday trader.

Journal

You have to maintain a journal where you will have to write down your daily experiences. This journal should help you keep track of your investments and tell you as to where your money has gone. You can invest in a digital diary or buy a physical journal.

These form the different things that you must do in order to start with your intraday investments on the right foot.

Chapter 3 Interest Rates

Exchange Rates and Interest Rates

Fluctuations in the interest rates of a nation also disturb its currency because of its effect on the Demand and supply of financial resources in the U.K. and abroad. For instance, high-interest rates compared to other countries make U.K. business-friendly to stakeholders, leading to higher Demand for U.K.'s financial resources and higher Demand for Pound Sterling.

On the other hand, lower interest duties in one country compared to other countries contribute to higher supply, as speculators sell currency to buy currencies connected with higher interest rates. Such hypothetical flows are called hot money and have an essential influence on exchange rates in the short run.

The Demand for Currency

The market for currencies is consequent from a country's Demand for exports, and from investors trying to benefit from currency value changes.

The Supply of Currency

The availability of a currency is determined by the domestic Demand for foreign imports. For instance, when the U.K. imports cars from Japan, they have to pay in yen and sell pounds to buy yen. The more it imports into the foreign exchange market, the larger the supply of pounds. A substantial proportion of short-term currency trading is by traders who work for financial institutes. The foreign exchange market of London is the single biggest currency exchange market in the whole world.

Supply and Demand

Supply and Demand run the foreign exchange (or Forex) market, much like every other market in the world. Indeed, knowing the idea of supply and Demand in the Forex market is so critical that we can take a step back into Economics 101 for a minute to make sure we're all on the same page. Having a firm knowledge of supply and Demand would make all the difference in your Forex investment career because it will give you the prospect to search through the daily news mountain and find the most exciting messages. And how does the Forex market is affected by both supply and Demand?

Supply is the indicator of how much of a given product at any particular time is accessible. The value of a product, in this case, a currency, is directly connected to its production. The currency would get less cost, with the currency supply rising. On the other hand, money becomes more valuable as the currency supply drops.

Think of diamonds and rocks. Since rocks are everywhere, they're not really useful. You can walk along a country path and pick from hundreds or even thousands of rocks. On the other side, diamonds are costly because many of them aren't on track. A limited volume of diamonds is available internationally, so if you like it, you have to offer a fee.

We find Demand, on the other hand, of the economic calculation. Demand is the indicator of how much customers desire to buy one particular product at any particular moment. Currency demand has the reverse impact on currency value than availability. The currency gets more expensive as the market for a currency rises. Alternatively, the currency is less competitive as Demand for a currency decline.

You just have to look at Tickle Me Elmo in order to get a clear sense of the impact demand may have on anything's price. Upon the first appearance of Tickle Me Elmo, the market for the product was insane. Parents trampled on each other so anyone else could wipe Elmo off their arms and make sure that they both got on their kid's list. To those not fast or competitive enough to bring Tickle Me, Elmo, from the market, it was their last resort to pay outrageously high rates on eBay. This giant red giggling doll had become a tremendous demand far more desirable than it would have been if it had been desired by no one's girl.

So, the trick to be effective in the currency market is to know about where the supply on the market is increasing and where Demand is rising. In this competitive industry, if you can choose that, you're well on your way to making a huge profit.

We consider utilizing the "seesaw of supply and demand" to show yourself a very good view of what is happening in the money market environment. And it is with one currency that influences each currency pair you are willing to exchange that is the best way to start this: U.S. dollar.

Chapter 4 Retail Vs Institutional Traders

etail traders are individuals who can be either part-time or full traders but don't work for a firm, and are not managing funds from other people. These traders hold a small percentage of the volume in the trade market.

On the other hand, institutional traders are composed of hedge funds, mutual funds, and investment banks who are often armed with advanced software, and are usually engaged in high-frequency trading.

Nowadays, human involvement is quite minimal in the operations of investment firms. Backed up by professional analysts and huge investments, institutional investors can be quite aggressive.

So at this point, you might be wondering how a beginner like you can compete against the big players?

Our advantage is the freedom and flexibility we enjoy. Institutional traders have the legal obligation to trade. Meanwhile, individual traders are free to trade or to take a break from trading if the market is currently unstable.

Institutional traders should be active in the market and trade huge volumes of stocks regardless of the stock price. Individual traders are free to sit out and trade if there are possible opportunities in the market.

But sadly, most retail traders do not possess the know-how in identifying the right time to be active and the best time to wait. If you want to be profitable in day trading, you need to eliminate greed and develop patience.

The biggest problem of losers in day trading is not the size of their accounts or the lack of access to technology, but their sheer lack of discipline. Many are prone to bad money management and over-trading.

Some retail traders are successful by following the guerilla strategy, which refers to the unconventional approach to trading derived from guerilla warfare. Guerilla combatants are skilled in using hit-and-run tactics like raids, sabotage, and ambushes to manipulate a bigger and less-mobile conventional opponent.

The US military is considered as one of the strongest armies in the modern world. But this mighty force suffered humiliation caused by the guerilla warfare used by North Vietnam during the Vietnam War.

Following this analogy, guerilla trading involves waiting or hiding until you are ready to grab an opportunity to win small battles in the financial warfare. This can help you gain fast revenue while minimizing your risk.

Remember, your mission is not to defeat institutional traders. Instead, you should focus on waiting for the right opportunity to earn your target income.

As a retail trader, you can make profits from market volatility. It can be impossible to make money if the markets are flat. Only institutional traders have the tools, expertise, and money to gamble in such circumstances.

You must learn how to choose stocks that can help you make fast decisions to the downside or upside in a predictable approach. On the other hand, institutional traders follow high frequency trading, which allows them to profit from very small price movements.

As a retail trader, you should only work in the retail domain The advantage of retail trading is that other retail traders also use them. The more traders use these strategies, the better they can work.

As more traders learn effective stock market strategies, more people will join the market so more stocks will move up faster. The more players in the market, the faster it will move. This is the reason why it is important for successful traders to share their strategies. This will not only help other traders to become more profitable, but it can also increase the number of traders who are using proven strategies.

There's no benefit in hiding these strategies or keeping them secret. In computer-aided trading, most of the stocks will follow the trend of the market, unless there's a good reason not to follow. Therefore, when the market is rising, most stocks will also move up. If the overall market is declining, the prices of the stocks will also decline.

But you should also bear in mind that there will be a handful of stocks that can go against the grain because they have a catalyst.

But for a brief overview, Alpha Predators are what retail traders are hunting for. These stocks usually tank when the markets are running, and they run when the markets are tanking.

It is generally okay if the market is running, and the stocks are running as well. Just be sure that you are trading stocks that are moving because they have a valid reason to move, and are not just moving with the general market conditions.

Probably, you are wondering what the basic catalyst for stocks is to make them ideal for day trading.

Here are some catalysts:

- Debt offerings
- Buybacks
- Stock splits
- Management changes
- Layoffs
- Restructuring
- Major contract wins / losses
- Partnerships / alliances
- Major product releases
- Mergers and / or acquisitions
- FDA approval / disapproval

- Earnings surprises

- Earnings reports

Retail traders who are engaged in reversal trades usually choose stocks that are selling off because there has been some bad press about the company. Whenever there's a fast sell-off because of bad press, many traders will notice and begin monitoring the stock for what is called a bottom reversal.

It can be difficult to perform a reversal trade if the stocks are trending down with the overall market like what happened to oil several years ago. The stock value increases by 20 cents and you may think it is a reversal. Then they are quickly sold off for another 60 cents. The sell-off is happening because the stocks are getting bad press.

For a while, oil was a weak sector and the majority of the energy and oil stocks were selling off. If a sector is weak, then it is not a good time for a reversal trade. This is where you need to identify the reason behind any significant movement in the market.

In order to do that, you need to remember the fourth rule in day trading:

Rule No. 4 - Always ask: is this stock moving because the general market is moving, or there's a unique catalyst behind this movement?

Research is crucial at this point. As you gain experience as a day trader, you will need to identify the difference between general market trends and catalyst-based movements. As a day trader, you need to be careful that you are not on the wrong side of the trade, and going against institutional traders.

How can you do that?

Stay away from trading stocks that are not getting enough attention. You will be in a sandbox doing your own thing. Go where everyone else is going. Concentrate on the stocks that are moving every day and are getting attention from retail traders.

Are blue-chip stocks like IBM, Coca-Cola, or Apple ideal for retail traders? You can try, but you need to remember that these are slow-paced stocks, which are heavily dominated by algorithmic traders and institutional traders. Plus, they are often very hard to trade.

How can you identify the stocks that are alluring retail traders? There are some proven ways to do this.

First, you can use day trading stock scanners. Basically, the stocks that are significantly moving up or down are the stocks that are being monitored by retail traders.

Second, find online community groups or social media groups where retail traders hang out. Twitter and Stock Twits are often good places to learn what is currently trending. If you regularly follow successful traders, then you may see for yourself what everyone is following. There's a big advantage to being part of a community of day traders.

You can read the insights of traders and the specific stocks they are considering. If you are a lone trader, then you may be out of touch in the market. You will just make it difficult for yourself because you will not know where the action is.

Chapter 5 Advantage And Negatives Of Day Trading

The first time I told my friends that I started day trading, I got two types of reactions: those who did not know anything about it thought that I was one of those big shots at Wall Street, who could be earning thousands or even millions of dollars every year. Meanwhile, those who had some understanding about investing and trading, since they were doing similar things themselves, probably thought I was a nut case.

Day trading is controversial. Some traders believe that it is a get-rich-quick scheme, and you know how people feel and think about that: the faster you climb, the quicker and harder you fall. In other words, while you gain something faster than you think, you also lose a lot in return.

They were concerned that I was about to lose my money—let me correct that. I think they believed that I would go bankrupt. Of course, I lost capital, but I did not have to file for bankruptcy.

Perhaps these people also do not understand the simple fact that day trading is not for everyone.

Advantage Of Day Trading

You should probably consider day trading if:

• **You want to earn profits at the end of the day.** The idea that it is a "get rich quick" scheme may be part truth since you do get to earn a profit after the market closes. For example, let us pretend that you invested $100 for 100 shares. The market fluctuation is in your favor so when you sell it you double your money, which means you now have revenue of $2 per share—not too shabby, right?

• **You want to think less about your investments.** This is because once the market closes, your trading also ends. Whether you win or lose, that is left to your skill and fate. The main point is that you will not have to think about whether your stock value will fall the next day or whether US dollar is going to be strong in the following week. You think day by day, moment by moment.

• **You can build cash inflow and liquidity very quickly –** This can be related to the first point. Because you can earn revenues and profits by the end of the day, you can also boost your assets, which then means you can buy more securities and increase your chance of earning more money in a short period of time. I highly encourage that you diversify your portfolio even if they belong to the same class (e.g. class of stocks) to protect yourself in deep market fluctuations, which are not that common anyway.

• **You are better protected against market fluctuations.** Okay, I mentioned just a while ago that diversification can help shield you from deep fluctuations in the market. But here is something to be happy about: the likelihood that it is going to dip extremely low is very small. As expected, market prices can change very fast in a blink of an eye, but the movements are often small.

- **You can be your own boss.** As a retail trader, you call the shots. You decide how much to invest, where to put your money, when to buy or sell, how much you like to earn, the securities you like to trade, etc.

- **You have help.** You may be a beginner, but the learning curve is not as difficult as it is with other securities or types of investing or trading. A variety of materials are available to make sure you do not have to trade blindly.

Negative Day Trading

If day trading is not as bad as others say, now why should I say it is not meant for everyone?

- **It requires a lot of time.** Okay, all types of work or endeavor needs it. I still have to find one that does not, and if it is legal and good, then I am definitely in. But when I say a lot, I truly mean it. You see, although there are specific hours of the day when you trade best, you still have to be alert as long as the market stays open because you will never really know what is going to happen. Stock prices could plunge, which gives you the perfect moment to buy blue chips or those that you can't afford before. If the European forex session is bad, there is a good chance US's session will suffer the same fate as well. It is almost the same scenario when we talk about other securities like bonds, hedge contracts, futures, or commodities.

Let us not forget too that you would have to do your research after or in between trading!

•   **It is risky.** To be honest, life is all about and related to risk. You are surrounded by it. When you cross the road or drive the car, you run the risk of meeting an accident. When you sleep, there is still a good chance you will never wake up! Have you heard of the term idiopathic? In science, it means a disease or a condition happens with no known or determined cause. It is simply saying it occurred just because it can.

The levels of risks we face on a daily basis, however, can vary. In the world of day trading, it can be on opposite ends, depending on how you trade and how much you put in. The bigger the money, the bigger the possible loss. The higher the returns, the higher the chance of falling hard. Losing is all part of the game. The problem comes in if you lose everything—that is a possibility, you know.

•   **It can make you emotional.** What has emotion got to do with day trading or any kind of trading for that matter? A whole lot than you can imagine. I remember the first time I earned a profit in day trading. It was not much, for someone who is just beginning, it meant something. I was so ecstatic I tried to trade more. Sadly, I lost the next day what I gained and traded. On the other hand, I know of friends who turn into monsters—angry, bitter, resentful, and irritable—once they begin trading. You can blame it on pressure, sense of competition, pride, or whatever. Whether you like it or not, day trading can get to you, and in many days, it is not a pleasant activity to do.

The relationship between emotions and commerce is strong. Many studies have already shown that customers are more likely to buy items on impulse and buy products that capture their emotions. The theory or concept of scarcity to sell something is also based on emotion. By instilling fear—the idea that if they do not act fast they can no longer take advantage of the offer—is what has earned several businesspeople millions or even billions of dollars.

You can therefore not avoid being emotional, whether it is positive or negative, when you are trading. However, you should learn how to control it and/or decrease its influence and impact on your decisions.

- **It can make you complacent.** These days it is so easy to get confident or even cocky with day trading. After all, you have more tools and resources compared to many years ago. You even have auto programs who can do the trading for you just in case you want have some me time in the middle of the day. But complacency can be one of your biggest mistakes. As you relax, that is when you become least prepared for the uncertainties. Your software can bog down, the analyses it provides you can be wrong, markets go down quickly without you knowing it—these things you could have resolved to minimize effect on you only if you have paid attention and be more proactive or do your part.

- **There are fees.** A lot of people think that they can just trade for free. Of course, it does not work that way. You have different expenses and fees to pay including commissions for every execution (e.g. buying or selling). And there are tax implications! Yup, you still have to pay your taxes because you are getting some profit from the transaction. In fact, taxes are higher for short-term investments such as those of day trading than the ones held for a long time, which is at least a year. But the good news is there are caps set. Also, if you're having a loss, you can write it off up to the amount of your capital gains. In cases where you have more losses than gains in a year, you can go beyond the amount of your capital gains and carry it over the succeeding year. For instance, for last year, you have 10,000 capital gains and $15,000 loss. You can zero your capital gains liability, leaving you with $5,000 more loss. You can then further reduce your tax liability by $3,000 and offset the next capital gains this year with $2,000. If you declare $18,000 capital gains this year, then your total liability is only $16,000.

Can You Do It for a Living?

Now that you know the advantage and negative parts of day trading, it's time that you answer the question: Can you do it for a living? By this, I mean you trade not just as a hobby or a one-time thing or an occasional gig. I mean you do it every day for as long as you can.

To help you answer that question, I have some more questions to ask:

• **Are you willing to invest money?** I am not just talking about hundreds or a couple of dollars. I am talking about thousands of them. As you go along the way, or as you trade for many years, you'll realize that you may be trading already a million dollars!

- **Are you ready to lose?** Between winning and losing, we definitely know what's a lot harder to take and get over with.

- **Are you ready to win?** Surprising question, isn't it? Why is it important for you to be ready for it? The answer is simple: I don't want you to be complacent. Haven't you noticed that when everything in your life is going well, you tend to forget about what's happening around you? You pay less attention to them because you think your life is so good it doesn't matter what is occurring around you anymore.

- **Are you willing to learn?** Many of my friends can attest that one of the beauties of day trading is the huge opportunity to earn and learn at the same time. I for one believe that you can't put a price tag on education even if it means committing mistakes first before you learn your lessons. You also need to learn too as the market is dynamic, and you need to change and grow along with it.

- **Are you ready to take the risks?** If you don't, then the immediate answer to the main question is big NO.

- **Are you willing to sacrifice?** Day trading requires commitment of your skill, time, effort, knowledge, and expertise. If you can't give a hundred percent of any of these to it, then you're not ready to make this a living.

Think about it.

Chapter 6 Types Of Trading

There are different reasons some traders love to use forex instead of the stock market. One of them is the forex leverage.

When it comes to forex trading, the entire system is totally different. Before you can trade using leverage, you need to have opened the forex trading account. That's the only requirement that is out there, nothing else. When you open a forex account, you can easily use the leverage feature.

If you are trading in the United States of America, you will be restricted to a leveraging of 50: 1 leveraging. Countries outside of the US are restricted to leverage of about 200: 1. It is better when you are outside the US, than in the US. Liquidity differences

When you decide to trade stocks, you end up purchasing the companies' shares that have a cost from a bit of dollars down to even hundreds of dollars. Usually, the price in the market tends to share with demand and supply.

Paired trades

When you trade with forex, you are facing another world, unseen in the stock market. Though the currency of a country tends to change, there will always be a great supply of currency that you can trade. What this means is that the main currencies in the world tend to be very liquid.

When you are in forex trading, you will see that the currencies are normally quoted in pairs. They are not quoted alone. This means that you should be interested in the country's economic health that you have decided to trade in. The economic health of the country tends to affect the worth of the currency.

The basic considerations change from one forex market to the next. If you decide to purchase the Intel shares, the main aim is to see if the stock's value will improve. You aren't interested in how the prices of other stocks are.

On the other hand, if you have decided to sell or buy forex, you need to analyze the economies of those countries that are involved in the pairs.

You should find out if the country has better jobs, GDP, as well as political prospects.

To do a successful trade in the Forex market, you will be expected to analyze not only one financial entity, but two.

The forex market tends to show higher level of sensitivity in upcoming economic and political scenarios in many countries.

You should note that the U.S. stock market, unlike many other stock markets is not so sensitive to a lot of foreign matters.

Price sensitivity to trade activities

When we look at both markets, we have no choice but to notice that there is varying price sensitivity when it comes to trade activities done.

If a small company that has fewer shares has about ten thousand shares bought from it, it could go a long way to impact the price of the stock. For a big company such as Apple, such n number of shares when bought from it won't affect the stock price. When you look at forex trades, you will realize that trades of a few hundreds of millions of dollars won't affect the major currency at all. If it affects, it would be minute.

Market accessibility

It is easy to access the currency market, unlike its counterpart, the stock market. Though you may be able to trade stocks every second of the day, five days weekly in the twenty first century, it is not easy.

A lot of retail investors end up trading via a United States brokerage that makes use of a single major trading period every day, which spans from 9: 30 AM to 4: 00 PM. They go ahead to have a minute trading hour past that time, and this period has price and volatility issues, which end up dissuading a lot of retail traders from making use of such time. Forex trading is different. One can carry out such trading every second of the day because there are a lot of forex exchanges in the world, and they are constantly trading in one time zone or the other.

Forex Trading Vs Options

A trader may believe the United States Dollar will become better when compared to the Euro, and if the results pan out, the person earns.

Chapter 7 Platforms And Broker

Platforms

If you are an experienced trader and you want to take a chance at taking on the market, you probably know what you want in a brokerage like comprehensive trading platforms, innovative strategy tools, premium research, and low costs. We have chosen some of the best brokers that you can use only in several different categories, so you will be able to choose one that is based on your personal priorities.

These next brokers have great pricing over their competitors and they have great trading tools and platforms:

Interactive Brokers and Options House have a powerful combination that each trader wants: Advanced trading tools and platforms paired with low commissions. Interactive Brokers tend to be the choice of traders that like per share pricing and is able to meet a minimum account of $10,000 with a minimum monthly commission of $10. This slightly affects their rating. Options House, on the other hand, gives traders a flat rate, and they don't require a minimum balance. The downside is they don't have forex trading. Interactive Brokers gives you access to forex, futures, and precious metals.

These brokers offer the most powerful platforms that are available without any fees or minimums:

Options House and Interactive Brokers have powerful platforms. Charles Schwab and TD Ameritrade also surpass others. TD Ameritrade probably has the best platform out there, think or swim, as well as Trade Architect that is very simple to use. Charles Schwab also gives you two great platforms: Streetsamrt.com is a great platform for beginners. Street-smart Edge is a more advanced functionality in charting. Both of which can be used by traders and they don't require any balance or activity minimums. Remember that there is an avoidable account minimum account balance of $1,000.

These brokers offer powerful tools and competitive pricing for options traders:

Trade Station and Options press are two more great options for traders to use. Which one you like the best will depend on what you are looking for in trade activity and platform needs. Trade Station is aimed more towards the professional trader. This platform will cost $99.95 each month, which is waived if you trade at least 5,000 shares, ten futures options or round-turn futures contracts, 50 options contracts, or carried a $100,000 balance. Trade Station's pricing is favorable to bulk traders, which give per-contract, flat fees, or volume discounts. Options Xpress don't require trade or account balance minimums, carry the extra fees, or offers competitive commissions, and they don't have vigorous trading. Trades with Options Xpress only cost $1.25 for each contract for traders who are active, and they have a $12.95 minimum charge for ten or fewer contracts

Traders that utilize margin needs to prioritize broker's margin rates while they search. These online brokers have the lowest margin rates:

None of the others can even come close to Interactive Brokers when you look at their margin rates. If margin rates are your priority, then this is a good option for you. This broker will charge you a grouped rate that is based on the balance of your account but also has a calculator to help traders to perform their math quicker. Interactive Brokers do have a minimum of monthly trade. E-Option's deposit requirement is a lot lower, and they have a more reasonable trade requirement. They only charge a $50 inactivity fee when you don't trade at least two times a year or who has less than $100,000 in debit or credit balances. Both of these options have competitive commissions for their options and stock trades.

Who Is A Broker?

This is someone who buys and sells goods or things on behalf of someone else. They mostly are middle men in transactions, that often they make profit out of. They only have to organize and plan for transactions to take place between a purchaser/buyer and a vendor/seller. The broker ends up getting a commission out of the deal, either from the buyer or seller. Most of the time they represent the seller.

Brokers may be individuals or firms. When it is a firm, it still acts as a go between their customer and the vendor.

Brokers exist in many different industries. An example would be real estate brokers who advertise and sell properties on behalf of the owners. We also have insurance brokers who sell insurance on behalf of firms. We have stock market brokers who work on the stock market.

Why Use A Broker?

There are a few advantages of using brokers in any kind of business. As usual, before getting into any business with a broker, always do intensive research on what you are about to get into. There are a few bad crops in the market.

They know their market well

Most brokers are people or firms who have been in the field for quite a while and always know what is best for one client to the other. They also know who to talk to if you need anything specific and always do it well knowing they will benefit.

Brokers have been on the market for a long time and have seen what goes on and know too well what to expect. They have all the information you need right from the time you enter the market to the time you leave. They are particularly important when you are entering a foreign market that you aren't familiar with. You need to take time and look for the perfect broker that will tell you what you need and how to do things the right way. However, you need to be wary of the brokers who are out to exploit you. Use referrals and other methods to try and get the right broker who understands your needs.

Wider representation

A client is able to reach more people or a wide marker when using a broker, compared to them doing it by themselves. Brokers are also quite affordable, and have a network they work with; hence there is limited cost incurrence with them. Because most of them are well known, they are able to reach a wider market ratio easily.

When you decide to work with a broker, you get to cast your net wider so that you can get better business. Coming up with a network takes time, which is why it is just right that you work with a person that already has a network which you can tap in. This saves you time and effort, as well as money. Take time to work with a broker that already has a network of established clients.

Special skills and knowledge

Brokers mostly have special knowledge of the field they are in and are good at the specific brokerage area. This is because they work in detail so as to know the needs of different types of clients. Because of this, they are an asset to anyone who is looking for their services.

The skills that a broker has vary from customer relationship management to money management. They will help you to grow your empire as you sit and wait for them to do the work you want. It takes experience and a lot of patience for you to learn the skills and be able to do the things that a broker can do. So, always make use of a broker when making trading decisions.

Customer choice

Brokers always work with the customer's choice. They will always want to know what one needs they will always endeavor to ensure the customer is satisfied and has what they originally wanted, or better.

Time saving

Because they mostly know their trade well, a broker would be able to achieve more within a shorter period of time for the customer. This is because of their great networking within their field of specialization. They always know where to find what, at what time and for what amount.

The time that you save when you work with a broker can be used to handle other tasks that you have. Take time to make sure the broker knows what they are doing otherwise you will end up wasting a lot of time.

Types of Brokers

- Stock broker
- Business broker
- Pawn Broker
- Information broker
- Insurance broker
- Investment broker

Chapter 8 What Is An Option Contracts

An options contract sounds fancy but it's a pretty simple concept.

•It's a contract. That means it's a legal agreement between a buyer and a seller.

• It gives the purchaser of the contract the opportunity to purchase or dispose of an asset with a fixed amount.

• The purchase is optional – so the buyer of the contract does not have to buy or sell the asset.

• The contract has an expiration date, so the purchaser – if they choose to exercise their right – must make the trade on or before the expiration date.

• The purchaser of the contract pays a non-refundable fee for the contract.

Suppose you are itching to buy a BMW and you've decided the model you want must be silver. You drop by a local dealer and it turns out they don't have a silver model in stock. The dealer claims he can get you one by the end of the month. You say you'll take the car if the dealer can get it by the last day of the month and he'll sell it to you for $67,500. He agrees and requires you to put a $3,000 deposit on the car.

If the last day of the month arrives and the dealer hasn't produced the car, then you're freed from the contract and get your money back. In the event he does produce the car at any date before the end of the month, you have the option to buy it or not. If you really wanted the car you can buy it, but of course, you can't be forced to buy the car, and maybe you've changed your mind in the interim.

The right is there but not the obligation to purchase, in short, no pressure if you decided not to push through with the purchase of the car. If you decide to let the opportunity pass, however, since the dealer met his end of the bargain and produced the car, you lose the $3,000 deposit.

In this case, the dealer, who plays the role of the writer of the contract, has the obligation to follow through with the sale based upon the agreed upon price.

Suppose that when the car arrives at the dealership, BMW announces it will no longer make silver cars. As a result, prices of new silver BMW is that were the last ones to roll off the assembly line, skyrocket. Other dealers are selling their silver BMW is for $100,000. However, since this dealer entered into an options contract with you, he must sell the car to you for the pre-agreed price of $67,500. You decide to get the car and drive away smiling, knowing that you saved $32,500 and that you could sell it at a profit if you wanted to.

The situation here is capturing the essence of options contracts, even if you've never thought of haggling with a car dealer in those terms.

An option is in a sense a kind of bet. In the example of the car, the bet is that the dealer can produce the exact car you want within the specified time period and at the agreed upon price. The dealer is betting too. His bet is that the pre-agreed to price is a good one for him. Of course, if BMW stops making silver cars, then he's made the wrong bet.

It can work the other way too. Let's say that instead of BMW deciding not to make silver cars anymore when your car is being driven onto the lot, another car crashes into it. Now your silver BMW has a small dent on the rear bumper with some scratches. As a result, the car has immediately declined in value. But if you want the car, since you've agreed to the options contract, you must pay $67,500, even though with the dent it's only really worth $55,000. You can walk away and lose your $3,000 or pay what is now a premium price on a damaged car.

Another example that is commonly used to explain options contracts is the purchase of a home to be built by a developer under the agreement that certain conditions are met. The buyer will be required to put a non-refundable down payment or deposit on the home. Let's say that the developer agrees to build them the home for $300,000 provided that a new school is built within 5 miles of the development within one year. So, the contract expires within a year. At any time during the year, the buyer has the option to go forward with the construction of the home for $300,000 if the school is built. The developer has agreed to the price no matter what. So if the housing market in general and the construction of the school, in particular, drive up demand for housing in the area, and the developer is selling new homes that are now priced at $500,000, he has to sell this home for $300,000 because that was the price agreed to when the contract was signed. The home buyer got what they wanted, being within 5 miles of the new school with the home price fixed at $300,000. The developer was assured of the sale but missed out on the unknown, which was the skyrocketing price that occurred as a result of increased demand. On the other hand, if the school isn't built and the buyers don't exercise their option to buy the house before the contract expires at one year, the developer can pocket the $20,000 cash.

Chapter 9 Call And Put Option On The Stock Market

Call Option

A call option comes with an expiration date. You can find options that expire in the current week, over the next few weeks to a month, out to several months to two year from the present date.

Why Invest in Call Options?

You buy a call option when you are bullish on a stock. In other words, you buy a call option when you are expecting the price of the underlying stock to rise. Theoretically, if you are buying a call option, you are hoping to buy shares of stock at the strike price, which you expect to be lower than the market price at some point.

So, let's say that a stock is trading at $99 a share. You could buy a call option with a strike price of $100 a share, if there is a consensus that the stock is going to see a significant rise in prices before the option expires. Say for the sake of example that the option costs you $1. Options prices are quoted on a per share basis, so that means you have to spend $100 to buy the option.

Now say that before the option expires, the share price goes up as expected, say to $103 a share. Now you have two possibilities. When the price of the underlying stock goes up, the value of the option contract goes up as well. Maybe the price of the option has risen to $1.50 per share, say. So, in that case, you can simply sell the option and take the $0.50 per share profit.

You can also choose to exercise the option. This means you can buy the stock at the strike price of $100 a share, even though the market price of the stock has risen to $103 a share. So, your total expense is now $101 a share since you paid $1 to buy the option (assuming zero commissions, which is reasonable these days). So now, you can turn around and sell the stock at $103 a share on the open market, earning yourself a profit of $2 a share. And in some cases, investors may decide to keep the stock that they have now been able to purchase at a discount.

Breakeven Price.

An important concept in options trading is the breakeven price. For a call option, the breakeven price is the strike price + the price paid to buy the option, on a per share basis. So, if you are buying an option with a strike price of $212 for $2.50, the breakeven price is simply $212 + $2.50 = $214.50. This means that the share price must rise to at least $214.50 before exercising the option even warrants consideration, otherwise you would be losing money as a buyer. For options sellers, the breakeven price is important to note as well. If you are selling to open call options, you don't have to worry if the market price of the stock stays at or below the breakeven price. In this example, a call options seller would be fine as long as the stock price stayed at or below $214.50.

The Call Seller.

An options contract goes on the market when a seller "writes" the contract. For retail traders (individual, small traders) you sell to open from a list of available options. So, you would find a call option with an expiration date and strike price that you like, and then you sell it using your brokerage software. There are three ways that you can sell a call option, the most basic way is to sell a covered call. To do this, you would need 100 shares of the underlying stock. Keep in mind that there is a risk you will lose ownership of the shares; in the event the option is exercised, and the shares are "called away" from you. But a carefully selected strike price and expiration date can lower your risk. The goal of selling a covered call option is to generate income from shares of stock that you own. Remember that the breakeven price is going to be something to keep your eye on in this case.

In those types of strategies, there is a single transaction involving multiple options that are bought and sold, and so using a strategy you are never going to be selling a single option.

Finally, you can sell a call option "naked", which means that you don't own the shares of stock. You must be a level four trader in order to sell naked options.

The call seller has a risk of assignment. That means, if the share price rises above the breakeven price, a buyer of an option may choose to exercise the option. As a seller you will be assigned and that means you will be forced to sell 100 shares of stock at the strike price. Many articles about options will assert that most options expire worthless, but the reality is if the option you have sold goes "in the money", there is a real risk that the option will be exercised. In fact, options that expire in the money are often automatically exercised by the broker. Check with your broker to find out their specific policies.

Profits from Call Options.

If you are buying call options, then you are hoping to make a profit from either exercising the option or simply selling it at a profit. Most beginning options traders are going to be working with smaller amounts of capital, and so you are probably not going to be interested in exercising the option. Rather, you are going to earn profits from the option itself. As the price of the underlying stock increases, the value of a call option increases as well.

There are several factors working in options pricing, and so you have to take more than just the underlying price of the stock into account. The most important of these is the expiration date. Simply put, the more time there is until an option expires, the more valuable it is. The value in the options price is referred to as time value, and it also makes up a part of "extrinsic" value of the option. With each passing day, the option will lose time value. At market open, that amount is automatically deducted from the options price. That doesn't mean you can't hold options overnight, because other factors will be operating to push up the price of the option as well, and this may overwhelm the decline in price from the loss of time value. This loss of time value is called "time decay".

The most important factor in the price of the option, therefore, is the underlying share price on the open market. For a call option, whenever the share price increases, the value of the option is going to increase. This happens most strongly for in the money options, but all call options will increase in value when there is a movement upward in the share price. So, you can even earn significant profits from out of the money options on a day when there are large upward movements in the price of the stock. These movements don't have to be particularly large; a single dollar rise in share price can mean anywhere from a $50 to $100 increase in the price of an option. So, you could buy an option in the morning and if the share price rises by a dollar during the day, you could sell it for a $50 to $100 profit. The more the share price rises, the more profit is possible. While out of the money options will often yield lower profit amounts for a given share price movement, the profits can still be substantial.

Put Option

Put options work in many ways in the same manner as call options. They have an expiration date, they have 100 shares of underlying stock, and their price depends on the price of the underlying stock. Meanwhile, they also suffer from time decay as the expiration date of the option approaches. However, put options actually gain value when the stock price drops, and they lose value when the stock price rises.

This means that put options can be used to "short" the stock. Shorting the stock is just jargon for earning a profit when the stock price declines. Normally, shorting a stock works like this. If you think that a stock is going to drop in value, you borrow shares from your broker – and you immediately sell them on the market at the current stock price. Then, assuming that your bet was the correct one, you buy the shares back when the price drops. Suppose for the sake of example that when you initially borrowed the shares, you sold them at $100 a share. Then the price drops to $80 a share – maybe the company had a bad earnings call, for example. When the price drops, you buy the shares back at $80 a share, and you return them to the broker (remember, you started the process by borrowing shares from the broker). This exercise leaves you with a $20 per share profit.

Of course, most small investors don't have $10,000 or more to chance on schemes like this, but put options enable you to earn profits if the price of a stock declines, using much smaller investments. The idea is basically the same, but when you suspect that the price of a stock is going to drop in the near future, you can buy put options on the stock. A put option has a strike price just like a call option, and when the share price is below the strike price, the put option is in the money. That's because you would be able to buy shares of stock at the market price, and then sell them at the strike price – earning a profit in the process.

Using the same example, we considered before, you could buy a put option with a $100 strike price. Then when the price of the shares dropped to $80, you could buy them on the market, and then sell them to the originator of the put option contract at the strike price - $100 a share. Buying a put option is something that doesn't require a large margin account to do.

When a put option is exercised, that is you sell the stock at the strike price, they say that the stock was "put to" the originator of the option contract. Of course, most options traders are not looking to exercise individual put options. If the stock price were really to drop $20 a share on a stock where you bought put options with a $100 strike price, the value of the put options would go up substantially, because you could exercise them and make solid profits. Since there are other traders who would be interested in selling the stock, you will be able to sell your put option to another trader for a profit. Remember that if you buy to open an options contract, you are not obligated to anything and are free and clear once you sell it to someone else.

Think of put options in the same way as call options, but with the price going up $100 every time the stock drops by $1. Like call options, the pricing of put options is impacted by many factors, and so this is an ideal relationship that we are thinking about here. But it gives you a rule of thumb to understand how put options work (the more in the money they are, the closer they are going to get to the ideal case). Likewise, if the price of the stock rises by $1, the value of a put option would move down by $100.

Chapter 10 Volatily In The Markets

Volatility is something that long-term investors ignore. It's why you will hear people that promote conservative investment strategies suggesting that buyers use dollar cost averaging. What this does is it averages out the volatility in the market. That way you don't risk making the mistake of buying stocks when the price is a bit higher than it should be, because you'll average that out by buying shares when it's a bit lower than it should be.

In a sense, over the short term, the stock market can be considered as a chaotic system. So from one day to the next, unless there is something specific on offer, like Apple introducing a new gadget that investors are going to think will be a major hit, you can't be sure what the stock price is going to be tomorrow or the day after that. An increase on one day doesn't mean more increases are coming; it might be followed by a major dip the following day.

For example, at the time of writing, checking Apple's stock price, on the previous Friday it bottomed out at $196. Over the following days, it went up and down several times, and on the most recent close, it was $203. The movements over a short-term period appear random, and to a certain extent, they are. It's only over the long term that we see the actual direction that Apple is heading.

Of course, Apple is at the end of a ten-year run that began with the introduction of the iPhone and iPad. It's a reasonable bet that while it's a solid long-term investment, the stock probably isn't going to be moving enough for the purposes of making good profits over the short term from trades on call options (not too mention the per share price is relatively high).

The truth is volatility is actually a friend of the trader who buys call options. But it's a friend you have to be wary of because you can benefit from volatility while also getting in big trouble from it.

The reason stocks with more volatility are the friend of the options trader is that in part the options trader is playing a probability game. In other words, you're looking for stocks that have a chance of beating the strike price you need in order to make profits. A volatile stock that has large movements has a greater probability of not only passing your strike price but doing so in such a fashion that it far exceeds your strike price enabling you to make a large profit.

Of course, the alternative problem exists – that the stock price will suddenly drop. That is why care needs to be a part of your trader's toolkit. A stock with a high level of volatility is just as likely to suddenly drop in price as it is to skip right past your strike price.

Moreover, while you're a beginner and might get caught with your pants down, volatile stocks are going to attract experienced options traders. That means that the stock will be in high demand when it comes to options contracts. What happens when there is a high demand for something? The price shoots up. In the case of call options, that means the stock will come with a higher premium. You will need to take the higher premium into account when being able to exercise your options at the right time and make sure the price is high enough above your strike price that you don't end up losing money.

Traders take some time to examine the volatility of a given stock over the recent past, but they also look into what's known as implied volatility. This is a kind of weather forecast for stocks. It's an estimate of the future price movements of a stock, and it has a large influence on the pricing of options. Implied volatility is denoted by the Greek symbol σ, implied volatility increases in bear markets, and it actually decreases when investors are bullish. Implied volatility is a tool that can provide insight into the options future value.

For options traders, more volatility is a good thing. A stock that doesn't have much volatility is going to be a stable stock whose price isn't going to change very much over the lifetime of a contract. So while you may want to sell a covered call for a stock with low volatility, you're probably not going to want to buy one if you're buying call options because that means there will be a lower probability that the stock will change enough to exceed the strike price so you can earn a profit on a trade. Remember too that stocks that are very volatile will attract a lot of interest from options traders and command higher premiums. You will have to do some balancing in picking stocks that are of interest.

Being able to pick stocks that will have the right amount of volatility so that you can be sure of getting one that will earn profits on short term trades is something you're only going to get from experience. You should spend some time practicing before actually investing large amounts of money. That is, pick stocks you are interested in and make your bets but don't actually make the trades. Then follow them over the time period of the contract and see what happens. In the meantime, you can purchase safer call options, and so using this two-pronged approach gain experience that will lead to more surefire success down the road.

One thing that volatility means for everyone is that predicting the future is an impossible exercise. You're going to have some misses no matter how much knowledge and experience you gain. The only thing to aim for is to beat the market more often than you lose. The biggest mistake you can make is putting your life savings into a single stock that you think is a sure thing and then losing it all.

Chapter 11 Day Trading And Swing Trading

The definition of day trading, which includes day traders keep their shares for the day. His posit they close their positions at the end of each day, and again the next day. On the other hand, they have a swing trader bonuses for days and sometimes even months; Investors are sometimes left for years. The short-term nature of the trading day reduced some risks because nothing can happen overnight, causing significant losses. At the same time, many other types of investors to go to bed thinking that his position is in perfect condition to wake up the next morning and discovered that the company announced huge profits or CEO is accused of fraud.

But there is another side (not always a disadvantage, right?): Select the values and positions that have to work a day trader or the day is done. Tomorrow does not exist for a given office. Meanwhile, swing trader or investor has the luxury of time, as it may take some time to get into the role they should. In the long run, markets are practical and efficient, and the prices reflect all information on the link.

Take a few days to realize efficiency.

Day traders are speculators, who work in a zero-sum market one day at a time. This makes the dynamics of various other types of financial activities that you can participate in. On the business rules, adoption day to help choose a good deed or to find significant investment funds in recent years are no longer used. Day Trading is a different game with different rules.

Hedgers and speculators. Speculators were looking to take advantage of price changes. Arbitrageurs try to protect themselves against price changes. They ensure that your choice of buying and selling are safe and cannot win. Therefore, select the elements that offset their exposure to another market.

For example, the cover should be considered as a food, a farmer who creates or increases the ingredients that the company needs. The Company may seek to hedge against the risk of rising prices of elemental components - like corn, oil and meat - purchase agreements with these ingredients. Therefore, if rates rise, corporate profits in contracts to help finance the rising costs will have to pay for these ingredients. If prices remain the same or fall, the company loses the contract price, which is the compensation for the company.

Secondly, it is beneficial if prices rise and suffer if they fall. To protect against falling prices, the farmer can sell futures contracts on these products. Their futures position to make money if the price dropped to compensate for a decrease in their products. And if rates rose, losing money on contracts, but the increase in its harvest offsets this loss.

The commodity markets were designed to help farmers manage risk and find buyers for their products. The equity and bond markets were created to encourage investors to finance businesses. Almost immediately, rumors ran in all these markets, but it was not his primary goal.

Day traders are speculators. They try to make money in the market as they are now. They manage risk by spreading wealth carefully, using stop orders and limit orders (positions predetermined price levels were reached as quickly as possible in the vicinity) and the sunset. They use other techniques to reduce losses, such as money management with caution and stop and limit orders.

Day Trading Strategies

Specify the number of things you need to become a reseller of the day is a good computer and Internet settings. They are necessary for the commercial success of the day. Most entrepreneurs have two or more monitors with integrated PC for managing a large number of data sources simultaneously. Windows XP or Vista is a popular form of day traders, as most trading platforms are written for these environments and can support multiple monitors.

Daily computer maintenance is essential for day traders. Computer problems are the last thing you want to live in the middle of the day, especially when long positions were opened. You can lose more money if you wait until the computer restarts and disappears store. Operators should delete cookies (files that websites send to your computer when used) Internet cache and defragment daily (change your data so that more effective teamwork).

Another critical step is to find an Internet provider that offers reliable service broadband (ISP). Many operators have more than one online service provider, so they have a backup in case the first serious.

The risk is high; Prices may be high.

A study of business models and wholesale volumes, you've probably already discovered for themselves that the risk is high. In minutes, enter and can be cumbersome for the shares in blocks of thousands of stocks quickly when the action moves in an unexpected direction.

The Senate of the United States considered the risk in trading the day after the shooting in a mall in Atlanta, Georgia, killing nine people in July 1999. Sniper Mark Barton was a chemist before engaging in day trading and only lose $ 105 000 per month. He committed suicide after injection.

Researchers found that the income of the Senate of the 15 largest companies trading in 1999 was $ 541.5 million, 276% more than their salary income in 1997 increased by more than 66 million in 2000, $ 15 businesses opened 12,000 new accounts. The researchers also found that the 4000 and 5000 most active traders have vast amounts of money and lose. Also, in 2000, buyers pay an average of $ 16 per transaction and an average of 29 sales per day. Using these statistics, the researchers concluded that the trader must win more than $ 111,000 per year for capital gains to offset the cost level.

The second study, published in May 2004 by university professors who analyzed the daily life of the Taiwan Stock Exchange, it was found that 82% of traders lost money.

You can do almost every day but ended up losing money after calculating operating costs.

Swing Trading

Swing trading is described as the art and science of making short term ranging from several days to several weeks or two months to get the most out of bond price movements. Swing traders may be individuals or institutions, such as hedge funds. Rarely 100% invested in the market at any time. Instead of waiting for low-risk opportunities and try to take the part of the significant lion movement up or down. When the demand is generally increasing, they buy more often they are short. When the market is usually low, which are shorter than buying. And if the market does keep away patiently.

Swing trading is different from the purchase and care or day trading. This approach of investors on the various frequencies trade market, and pay particular attention to the different data sources. You must understand that these differences do not focus on issues that have an impact on long-term investors.

One of the highlights of the action is the efficiency with which they are traded, in part because they provide exposure to other asset classes. For example, you can get exposure to the assets of gold products marketing funds trading gold. Guard things about yourself, because that is my area of expertise, and also recommended after exposure to other asset classes and a variety of items that you can select.

American Depositary receipts (ADR): ADR is increasingly essential in today's globalized world. In simple terms, we ADR allows investors to buy shares of foreign companies. Adverse reactions are denominated in US dollars and the payment of dividends in US dollars. Exchange ADR is much more cost-effective than creating accounts in various other countries to convert their dollar, etc. And as economic growth in developing countries is higher than in developed countries, ADR can be substantial profit opportunities. ADR markets-based companies (such as Brazil and China) emerging sometimes have a significant impact on a particular product, allowing them to benefit from high commodity prices.

Exchange-Traded Funds (ETFs):

Investments. Most courses ETF reflects the movement of the index (by famous ETF SPY following example the S & P 500) index or sub-sector. If you want to enjoy the technology of the future will be better able to negotiate the selection of specific techniques, Technology ETF that may or may not be in the area of global technology. If you travel, you will have a diversified technology ETF. However, only safety technology can resist the trend. ETFs also offer the ability to use indices and international products.

The closed funds: These funds are mainly traded funds on the secondary value of equity investments. Traditional investment funds and open-end are valued based on their net worth - or the amount left after deducting the liabilities of the fund's assets. Closed-end funds are different. Its price is determined by supply and demand of shares of the fund. Sometimes the lower closed change of the NAV; at other times, to negotiate less. Closed-end funds can be an effective way to tap international markets.

Debt markets: These markets include bonds issued by governments at the federal, state and local, as well as those issued by companies. The value of fixed income securities depends on interest rates, inflation, the creditworthiness of the issuer and other factors—the bond market generally less volatility than equities and other asset classes.

Chapter 12 Candlestick

Price action

I t is no secret that the main thing involved in a stock market is "price fluctuation". It is the rise and fall of the stock prices that makes it possible for the trader to break into a profit, or suffer a loss. So to remain successful, the trader has to predict the price rise and fall successfully. This can be done through a method known as price action. Price action is conducted by taking into account the various prices that the stock has held over a period of time along with other data, statistics and mathematical formulas that are applied in order to arrive at the price fluctuation rate and range. This will help the trader make accurate speculations and realize profit whilst minimizing losses. However, as good as it sounds, the formulas that are used are extremely complex and the average person might not be able to do it easily.

Bullish candlesticks

Candles that have a larger body towards the top are considered bullish, and they mean that the buyers will be the ones who are in control of the price. When you see this kind of chart, realize that it is likely that the buyers will keep pushing so that the price goes higher. This kind of candlestick is not only going to tell you the price, but it is also able to tell you that the bulls are winning and that they have the power.

Bearish candlesticks

There are also the bearish candles. They will work a bit differently than you will find with the bullish candlesticks and can have you react in a different manner. When you see a bearish candle, it means that the sellers are the ones in control of the price action that goes on in the market and that buying would probably not be a good idea at this time.

When you see a candle that is filled and has a pretty long filled body, it means that your opening was high, but the closing was low. This is one way to tell that the market is bearish right now and it is probably not a good idea to get into the market at this time. You will probably not get a good price for the stocks because the market price is going down and there are not as many buyers interested right now.

Just by being able to read these candlesticks, you will be able to generate an opinion for how the stock will generally, or the price action. You need to understand which party (the buyer or the seller) is in charge of the price can help you determine whether now is a good time to purchase the stock or not. When you have a bullish market, the price will keep going up, so it is a good idea to jump in and then sell the stock at a higher price. But if you are in a bearish market, the price is most likely going to go down, and it is not in your best interest to make a purchase.

Indecision candlesticks

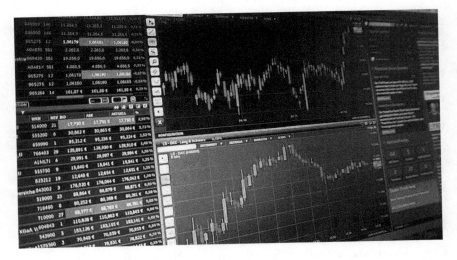

There are also some candlesticks that are known as indecision candlesticks. There are two main types of indecision candlesticks including spinning tops and Dojis. Let's take a look at these and determine what they both mean for the market.

Spinning tops

The spinning tops are candles that have the high wicks that are similarly sized and then low wicks that happen to be larger than the bottom and look a bit indecisive. With these candlesticks, the sellers and the buyers have powers that are pretty close to even. No one is really in control over the price of the stock, but there is still a fight that is going on. The volume on these will be lower because the traders want to wait and see whether the buyers or the sellers will be the ones that wend.

You will notice that a trend in the price is often going to change right away after this kind of indecision candle, once the fight has been won by either the sellers or the buyers, so it is worth your time to recognize this kind of price action. You may want to wait a bit before jumping into the market to see which way the market will go. Sometimes it will go well, and the price will go up, but the market could also go the other way, and you could see the price drop.

Dojis

Another type of candlestick pattern that you should watch out for is the Doji. There are actually a few forms and shapes of this, but they are either going to have no body to the candlestick or at least a really small body. When you see that there is a Doji in the chart, it means that there is a fight that is going on between the bulls and the bears and no one is winning yet.

There are some times when the Doji will have a bottom and top wick that are unequal. If the top of the wick ends up being longer, it means that the buyer tried to get the price higher, but they were unsuccessful. They may show that the buyers are starting to lose power and it is possible that the sellers may start to take over. On the other hand, if the bottom wick is longer, this means that the sellers tried to push the price down and they were not successful. This may mean that there will be a takeover of the price action by the bulls.

You can definitely use this to help you see what trends are going on. If one of these candlesticks shows up during a bullish trend, it means that the bulls are wearing out and now the bears are trying to take over control of the price. If this candlestick forms when there is a bearish downward trend, it suggests that now the bears are tired and now the buyers or the bulls will take over the price. This can help you to see when a trend is about to occur in the market and can help you to make some smart decisions.

The candlestick pattern is a great way to predict how the market is going. When the market is going up based on these candlesticks, you will want to purchase and then sell before they go down. When the market is going down based on these candlesticks, you will either want to stay out of the market if you are not already in, or you will want to sell before the price goes down and you lose too much money. Take some time to learn how to make these charts, and you will find that they are a fantastic way for you to monitor the way that the market is going.

Candlesticks patterns

The "candlestick" pattern is best suited for people who would like to adopt a technical approach and trade based on patterns and predictions. The "candlestick" pattern involves the creation of patterns for particular stocks based on its "LOD" or lowest of the day and "HOD" or highest of the day prices. Depending on these statistics, the graph is plotted. There is a technique known as the doji reversal pattern that helps in establishing proper "candlesticks". Once the "candlesticks" have been established, the trader will be able to identify the pattern that the stock will follow. Once it has been established, he will predict whether the price will rise or plummet. Depending on the prediction the trader will decide to either hold on to the stock or sell it off. This technique is easy to follow if you understand the technique properly and for that.

Chapter 13 Day Trading Strategies

ABCD Pattern

The ABCD trading pattern is a relative of the Elliot Waves in the sense that it is based on the fact that the market moves in an organized manner. In addition, it is one of the most profitable day trading strategies that you can find out there. Since the pattern is based on pure price action and follows market structure, it is a powerful leading indicator.

Structure

The pattern uses impulse and corrective waves to predict the future of the market. The points named A, B, C, and D represent significant highs and lows in the market. When points A and B are joined, they form a wave known as a "leg." As such, the pattern is made up of legs AB, BC, and CD, where AB and CD are impulse waves, and BC is a corrective wave. AB and CD should be parallel to each other. We predict the future of the market by placing trades at the end of leg CD and in the direction of BC.

- Leg AB is equal to Leg CD in the "classic ABCD" pattern.

- Leg CD can extend by 127.2% or 161.8% in the "ABCD extension" pattern.

•	The time it takes to form AB is the same it should take to form CD in the "Classic ABCD" pattern.

•	Leg BC is the corrective wave and gives the direction of reversal after the completion of the leg CD.

Before we go any further into this pattern, we need to discuss an important tool that should be used alongside the pattern for better analysis. It is called the Fibonacci sequence tool.

Classic ABCD Pattern

•	The length of AB is equal to the length of the leg CD

•	The time it takes to form AB is the same it takes to form CD

•	Point C should not go near point A. Similarly, point D should not be near point C. In short, you should have clear swing points indicating a good trend.

•	The leg BC should retrace to 127.2% or 161.8% of BC. To plot this, since we have an uptrend, the Fibonacci would be drawn from point B (swing high) up to point A (swing low). Then as the market unfolded, it would bounce off C (retracement level) and continue to create leg CD. Once the trader is sure that the classic ABCD has completed, they can enter a sell trade at point D (reversal into a downtrend).

Extended ABCD Pattern

An extended ABCD pattern is different from the classic ABCD pattern in that the leg CD can be longer than leg AB by between 127.2% and 161.8%. Also, the time that it takes to form CD can extend by the same percentages.

Trading With the ABCD Pattern

You can add some of the other tools like support & resistance to your ABCD pattern trading style to improve the accuracy of the turning points. The stronger a zone is, the more likely that your leg is accurate. Fibonacci levels also work well when combined with support & resistance zones. Confluence at turning points or entry points can be increased by utilizing the knowledge of candlestick formations or a few indicators. However, be careful not to have too many tools in your charts as this can lead to analysis paralysis.

It is very important that you always keep in mind that no trading strategy is foolproof. You might have the best analysis and find the most promising trade signals, but still, the market might ignore and oppose you. Therefore, to be safe from excess losses, make sure to always have a protective stop-loss order immediately after you place a trade. The ABCD pattern makes stop-loss placement very easy. You need to identify a zone below or above point D and place it there. The First Take-Profit Level can be placed at the level of C. You can have a Second Take-Profit Level at point A or where your Fibonacci extension level coincides with strong support or resistance level.

Bull Flag Momentum

A bull flag is a strong upward trend in the stock. However, after shooting upward, the stock enters a phase of consolidation, when people slow down or stop buying, but before a new rise may begin. The "flag pole" is a steep rise in the price of the stock over a very short time period. The "flag" is a time period when the price is high but stays about the same. A bull flag is a symbol of a buying opportunity for a stock that has already shown a significant increase. You should set your desired profit, buy and then sell when it begins increasing again up to the point where you have set to take your profit. You should always include a stop-loss, a bull flag is no guarantee and the price might actually start dropping.

When there is a bull flag, it is bordered along the bottom by a level below which the stock is not dropping, known as the support. On the top, there is a level above which the stock is not rising. This is called resistance. Eventually, the stock is going to break out of the resistance so you want to buy before this happens, as the stock may see a rapid rise again. A bull flag may occur multiple times during the day as the stock trends upward.

Reversal Trading

A reversal is a major change in the direction of the price of the stock. So, the trend completely shifts and moves in the opposite direction. In order to look for reversals, look at the candlesticks on a stock market chart. The body of the candlesticks and its size relative to the previous (to the left) candlesticks is what is important. First, let's consider a signal for a reversal where a declining stock price is going to be going up in the future. If the candlestick of the most recent time is larger and fully engulfs or covers the candlestick to the left, and it's the opposite color, i.e. a green candlestick following red candlesticks, this indicates a reversal of a downtrend into an increasing stock price. This is a good time to go long or buy calls.

On the other hand, let's now consider the case where the stock price is going up, with multiple green candlesticks in a row. Then it is followed by an engulfing red candlestick. This indicates a reversal so we will expect the stock price to begin going down. That is, this is a point where we should short the stock, or if trading options invest in puts.

The larger the engulfing candlestick, the stronger the reversal signal is. That indicates that the change in direction has a significant conviction behind the reversal, which is the confidence of investors, larger volume and the price will change in larger amounts over short time periods. If the wicks engulf the wicks of the previous period that is an even stronger signal that a reversal is underway.

When using reversals as a trading strategy, you need a minimum of five candlesticks in a five-minute chart. Then look at the relative strength index, which helps you evaluate overbought or oversold stocks. The RSI ranges from 0-100. At the top of an uptrend, if the RSI is above 90 that indicates that the stock is overbought and is probably going to be heading into a downturn. On the other hand, if you are looking at the bottom of a downturn, if the RSI is 10 or below, this indicates that the stock is oversold. That could be a signal that is about to see a price increase.

An indecision candlestick indicates neither an upturn nor a downturn. That is if you see a downturn followed by several indecision candlesticks, that could mean that the stock is about to turn upward again. Or vice versa – if an upturn is followed by several indecision candlesticks, that can indicate a reversal resulting in a downward trending stock price.

Looking at the wicks can be important as well. When the lower wick of the candlestick is longer, that may indicate that the price dropped over the period of the candlestick, but the stock turned and was bought up. On the other hand, if the candlestick has a long wick at the top that may indicate that the stock was bid up too much over the period. Traders lost interest and began selling off the stock.

At any time, there appears to be a reversal, a trend of indecision candles or stagnation represents a buying opportunity no matter which direction the stock may be trending. That is if you are in the midst of a downturn and the stock is moving sideways, then it may be a good time to go long on it or buy calls. The opposite is true if the stock is at the top of a potential reversal. If it's moving sideways, it may be a good time to invest in puts. Keep in mind that this does not always work. The best indicator is whether or not a green (red) candlestick following a red (green) candlestick which engulfs the candlestick to the left is the best indicator of a coming reversal.

Support or Resistance Trading

In order to understand the meaning of support and resistance levels, one needs a clear background check on what day trading entails. Day trading is the process of having a forecast in securities. This involves the purchase and sale of financial instruments within the same day of trading. The closure of business here is dependent on the end of the business day. Trading in this kind of manner is based on speculation. The probability of profit and loss is not defined. Owing to this, you may experience losses and profit in any instance. For one to engage in this type of trade and survive, one needs a well-structured strategy that will ensure you are speculating the right way. In a nutshell, day trading can be referred to as the acquisition or disposal of securities within a single trading day. The background of day traders is one that is full of funding and well-conversant with the business field. Their game is fixed on short-term strategies that have a high value of leverage. In this sense, they tend to capitalize on shifts in prices no matter how remote it may seem.

Day traders thrive on events that cause shifts in price. This is usually in the short term. The news is their biggest asset. Trading in the news will ensure that they have information concerning market psychology. This includes the announcement on various interest rates, statistics, market expectations, and corporate earnings. Day traders employ numerous strategies in their day to day activities.

These strategies include but are not limited to High-frequency trading, range trading, scalping and news based trading. The idea of day trading is fixed behind the misconception of getting rich quickly. Thus within a short period of time. This is often what attracts people to engage in this kind of trading. People who engage in this kind of trading without sufficient knowledge often end up in losses. Despite the risky nature in the manner of speculation that characterizes day trade, it is a lucrative business that puts food on the table for many lads. Its risky nature is what makes it so lucrative.

Behind every success story, there is a significant struggle story. People who engage in day trading have a view of making a profit. However, this is not always the case as some people result in irreparable loss. Before engaging in this particular type of trade, one needs an inner understanding of the factors at hand. The probability of making a profit is often lower.

Chapter 14 How To Do Day Trading With Option

The simplistic meaning of an underlying financial derivative is an alternative. A civil arrangement gives you the right to buy or sell an item on or during a specified date the date of exercise. If you are the vendor, you are obliged to agree with the terms of the contract. It will be either selling or purchasing if the customer wants to exercise the right before the expiry date. Day trading options cover multiple markets. You will get equity options, options for the ETF, options for futures, and more. Also named vanilla options are such conventional alternatives. The simplistic meaning of an underlying financial derivative is an alternative. A civil arrangement gives you the right to buy or sell an item on or during a specified date the date of exercise.

They can be practiced from the date of acquisition before expiry at any point. However, European options can only be exercised after the expiry date. Options vs Futures There are many differences between day trading options and futures that many people quickly know. They are normally both based on the same instrument that underlies them. There are also several parallels to the structure of the real contracts. The distinction is how the trade takes place. You get a wider range of options with the packages.

There are various reasons you might make serious trading opportunities for capital. For some enticing factors, including placing financial remuneration on the side, day trading of options appeals. Greater Advantages You can benefit even more from an option as the stock moves. But a call option going from $1 per contract to a $5 contract will offer you a benefit of 500 percent. And with an alternative, you will earn more and with less time. Options can be successful when other markets struggle. Although other business segments struggle, options can be successful. Partly because you don't have to use the right to make the best of it.

Besides, uncertainty can be positive for itself. Mutually beneficial – while stock options are often built on, add both and can offer you more benefits. That is because you can sell the income-generating right on stocks you already own. The trading of intraday options is multifaceted and carries tremendous opportunities for benefit with it. Perhaps the best aspect-usability. You can continue day-trading from anywhere in the world with options. What you need is to connect to the internet. Day trading and long-term investing are also feasible ways of stock trading and many traders are preferring to do so. Day trading means making trades that last for seconds or minutes, profiting from short-term swings in the price of an asset. Both accounts are opened and closed for day trading on the same day.

Understanding Margin

Day trading usually uses leverage margin during the day of trade. The margin rates and conditions differ according to the financial instrument of the Stock Margin and the broker. Day trading buying power for stocks and options has a lending ratio of 4 to 1 or four times the account's investment margin excess. In a simplistic way, that means that with the extra cash in the portfolio, you can buy stocks and options at just 25 percent of the market. Profit surplus is the norm to have client equity below debt. The overnight margin is between 2 and 1 or 50 percent of the value of the position.

Day traders can fall into traps if they don't know the profit is solely at the broker's discretion. Brokers will reduce the portfolio leverage ratio to 2 to 1, allowing 50 percent instead of 25 percent surplus equity for highly volatile stocks. This is a big consideration when initiating an intraday margin call. The broker is entitled to unwind a stake, frequently at the lowest times, when a margin call has to be reached. Stockbrokers can encourage traders to manipulate their cash and maximize their purchasing power intraday.

Chapter 15 How To Do Day Trading With Swing Trading

S wing trading comes with different opportunities and also frequent scares. These trades are made in shaky markets, and any time the market can crash with all those dollars invested in it.

Its advantage is that it uses longer time frames to track; therefore, one can manage a full-time job as opposed to the shorter time frames on day trading. So to avoid any pitfalls, one is advised to try it on a demo account first while learning the ropes. While swing trading, do not need to keep worrying about the trades that you made. The long time frame allows you to easily pursue other things as you wait to conduct your trade. Such a trade is very convenient since it gives room for flexibility. You would like a trade that gives you freedom. You find that you do not need to keep worrying about the moves that you make since you feel secure in your deals. As a trader, you would like to engage in a deal that grants you your freedom. You want to be at a point where you can carry out your other activities as you keep trading. In this case, swing trading will act as a side job that earns you an income. You get to do other things as you conduct swing trading. It is more like killing two birds with one stone.

Swing trading is also best experienced once one has mastered the art of money management so that you can project your profits wisely. This advanced time on the market will help you identify the patterns in the stocks, and this will improve your decision-making ability. In any business investment, the management of money matters a lot. We have had some businesses start out really well and ended up failing. You will be amused that they do not fail due to the lack of a good strategy. Instead, they fail due to poor management of finances. Any business that looks forward to making more profits, as the years advance, needs to look at how they manage their finances keenly. We have heard of cases where businesses started out well only to end up failing before making bigger strides. Money laundering has affected many businesses to the point of closure. Once you know how to engage in swing trading, ensure that you manage your finances. This will ensure that you make better decisions while carrying out various trades. With a good money management strategy, it gets easier to make progress in swing trading. You find that you will easily double your profits with this strategy.

Due to the longer time frames, have a reliable mode of communication as one is bound to forget to make moves on the market, thus ending up with huge losses. Timing is important in all the business deals that you engage in. The interesting thing about most motivational talks is how they insist on proper time management. You have probably come across some people that would prefer you to waste their money but not their time. The importance of time lies in the impact that it has on an individual. The time factor is also necessary while conducting various trades. Ensure that you are keen on the decisions that you make.

For instance, with the long durations in which the trades are carried out, you may forget the time you were required to trade. You find that you have a lot going on and keeping certain dates becomes a challenge. To avoid this, you can set a reminder on when you need to trade. At times, this will require that you are disciplined in carrying out your various activities. The decisions that you make, no matter how small, hold a big impact in your possibility of succeeding. Utilizing this strategy will help you a lot while trading options. It ensures that you are disciplined in keeping time and you trade in moments when you can get a big profit.

Observe the trends in the market and steer clear of trading with the trend. This is because its longevity might be questionable and therefore having a stock that fazed out while you were not tracking it is detrimental. Avoid trading against the most appealing trend and exercise caution by withholding yourself. As a trader, you need to be keen on how the market moves. You cannot achieve success in a certain area unless you fully understand what it entails. As an individual intending to engage in swing trading, one of the best strategies that you can utilize is knowing how the market operates. You will be surprised by the power of having information. In the world that we currently live in, ignorance will cost you a lot. Nowadays, information is readily available to us that one has no excuse not to learn.

In this era, the internet has done more good than harm to us. You can easily get any information that you want by conducting a simple search. We also have numerous resources within our reach that help us in acquiring the information that we would like. With the many resources, we certainly do not have any excuse for not having the knowledge that we need. Additionally, while learning, we can never completely finish learning everything. Each day comes with its own new things, and we need to embrace that. Have a positive attitude towards learning and see the impact it will have on conducting swing trades.

Swing trading allows for different skill sets in the trading as it takes a while for the stocks to exit the market. During this time, the beginner can go over whatever steps he would have forgotten in order to fortify his trading process. Asides from knowledge, we need to gain skills that help us in conducting different trades. These skills make the trading process easier. The difference between the people who succeed at certain things, and those that fail lies in the extra mile that they are willing to take. How hungry are you for success? What extra miles are you willing to make to get to a place that you would like to be? Your response to these questions can tell a lot about the kind of individual that you are. You find that successful people tend to be driven by their ambitions.

This does not only apply in other aspects of life, but it is also applicable in swing trading. There are many decisions that you will make, that will influence your general outcome. To become a good trader, you will have to come up with some tactics and strategies that make the trades manageable. Some people tend to view it as a complex thing, yet it is very easy to come up with tactics and strategies. The only thing that you will need is having adequate knowledge of how swing trading operates. Once you have the information, it is easy to come up with the strategies.

Know what stocks you are trading by keeping up with the latest using newspapers, financial markets and trade events. Use reliable sources to keep you up to tabs with the general markets and the high flying financial players. As the market expands, there is more to learn. We need to constantly keep up with the changing terms and factors influencing the market. It is a good thing that there are plenty of resources that we can utilize to have the information that you need. When you utilize this strategy, it allows you to be well informed. You find that you will even find it possible to make better decisions.

Be mentally prepared to make losses as much as you are prepared to make profits. This is an inevitable step in the trading process. Day trading is unpredictable as a stock can crash at any time during the day. This strategy has been a challenge for most people. You find that you are not open to the possibility of incurring a loss. Asides from the fact that the main purpose of investing is earning a profit, you have to be open to the challenges that come with investments. At times trades go contrary to what we expected. A single mistake can cause you to encounter a loss. At times, we have no control over some factors, and once we encounter a loss. While you engage in day trading, know that you can either win or lose at the end of the day. This will protect you from stress and other challenges that result from being stressed. You get to appreciate your efforts despite failing since you understand that failure is part of the success journey. Not every person can do this, but we need to encourage ourselves.

The time invested must be more than any other investment. The individual must set aside enough time to track and chart the stocks in order to see their performance and enable him to exit at the opportune time.

Use the percent rule in terms of funds. You must be willing to lose a bit so as to gain a lot in the financial markets. Some stocks are liable to burn while others are clear wins. At times we are advised that we need to part with money to make money. As we aspire to get rich, there are some major decisions that we will need to make. At times it will involve making sacrifices to get to the levels and positions that we aspire to be in. the path to success is not an easy journey, but we have to be fully committed to the process.

Learn how to time your trades. Even after getting on the market, allow some time to pass so as to see the stocks that are going to remain so as to avoid the volatile trends. During this time, you will have enough time to observe the patterns and allow for a window to make profits.

Avoid being enticed by buying so many stocks at once. Start small and get a maximum of two stocks that are easily managed within the small time frame that day trading provides. You are also likely to get more opportunities with these few stocks on the market. At times we have a misguided belief that the more stock one has, the more money they are likely to have. Contrary to this belief, one can make a loss while using such a strategy. Buying multiple stocks results in overtrading, and you may end up having overleveraged accounts. As a beginner, start with manageable stocks that you can handle. This allows you to evaluate the various stocks before purchasing them easily. You get to know the stocks that can earn you a profit as you avoid the stocks that will not help you in generating an income. Some expert traders are also unable to conduct multiple trades since they know the challenges that come with trading. This should show you how risky it is and help you avoid engaging in such. Ensure that you only engage in trades that you can manage so that you make wise decisions.

Be realistic about your profits and stick to the percentage rule so as to maximize your profits in the trade. Plan your exit strategy based on the profits you make and then leave. The high expectations that one has at the beginning makes them think that they can make money quickly. Sadly, day trading is not a plan to quickly earn an income. With this attitude, you will have major frustrations and disappointments. In the beginning, be patient enough to start small. You will grow as you proceed. The same way a child develops from childhood to adulthood in the same way that you can experience growth while day trading. It will take some time until you have the adequate skills to carry out trades successfully.

Chapter 16 Essential Tool For Day Trading

For you to carry out day trading successfully there are several tools that you need. Some of these tools are freely available, while others must be purchased. Modern trading is not like the traditional version. This means that you need to get online to access day trading opportunities.

Therefore, the number one tool you need is a laptop or computer with an internet connection. The computer you use must have enough memory for it to process your requests fast enough. If your computer keeps crashing or stalling all the time, you will miss out on some lucrative opportunities. There are trading platforms that need a lot of memory to work, and you must always put this into consideration.

Your internet connection must also be fast enough. This will ensure that your trading platform loads in real-time. Ensure that you get an internet speed that processes data instantaneously to avoid experiencing any data lag. Due to some outages that occur with most internet providers, you may also need to invest in a backup internet device such as a smartphone hotspot or modem. Other essential tools and services that you need include:

Brokerage

To succeed in day trading, you need the services of a brokerage firm. The work of the firm is to conduct your trades. Some brokers are experienced in day trading than others. You must ensure that you get the right day trading broker who can help you make more profit from your transactions. Since day trading entails several trades per day, you need a broker that offers lower commission rates. You also need one that provides the best software for your transactions. If you prefer using specific trading software for your deals, then look for a broker that allows you to use this software.

Real-time Market Information

Market news and data are essential when it comes to day trading. They provide you with the latest updates on current and anticipated price changes on the market. This information allows you to customize your strategies accordingly. Professional day traders always spend a lot of money seeking this kind of information on news platforms, in online forums or through any other reliable channels.

Financial data is often generated from price movements of specific stocks and commodities. Most brokers have this information. However, you will need to specify the kind of data you need for your trades. The type of data to get depends on the type of stocks you wish to trade.

Monitors

Most computers have a capability that enables them to connect to more than one monitor. Due to the nature of the day trading business, you need to track market trends, study indicators, follow financial news items, and monitor price performance at the same time. For this to be possible, you need to have more than one processor so that the above tasks can run concurrently.

Classes

Although you can engage in day trading without attending any school, you must get trained on some of the strategies you need to succeed in the business. For instance, you may decide to enroll for an online course to acquire the necessary knowledge in the business. You may have all the essential tools in your possession, but if you do not have the right experience, all your efforts may go to waste.

Chapter 17 Huge Mistakes That Beginners Make

Aside from doing the right things, you'll also need to refrain from certain things to succeed as a day trader. Here are some of the most common day trading mistakes you should avoid committing.

Excessive Day Trading

By excessive, I mean executing too many day trades. One of the most common mistakes many newbie day traders make is assuming that they can become day trading ninjas in just a couple of weeks if they trade often enough to get it right. But while more practice can eventually translate into day trading mastery later on, it doesn't mean you can cram all that practice in a very short period of time via very frequent day trading. The adage "the more, the merrier" doesn't necessarily apply to day trading.

Remember, timing is crucial for day trading success. And timing is dependent on how the market is doing during the day. There will be days when day trading opportunities are few and far between and there'll be days when day trading opportunities abound. Don't force trades for the sake of getting enough day trades under your belt.

Even in the midst of a plethora of profitable day trading opportunities, the more the merrier still doesn't apply. Why? If you're a newbie trader, your best bet at becoming a day trading ninja at the soonest possible time is to concentrate on one or two day trades per day only. By limiting your day trades, to just one or two, you have the opportunity to closely monitor and learn from your trades.

Can you imagine executing 5 or more trades daily as a newbie and monitor all those positions simultaneously? You'll only get confused and overwhelmed and worse, you may even miss day trading triggers and signals and fail to profitably close your positions.

Winging It

If you want to succeed as a day trader, you need to hold each trading day in reverence and high esteem. How do you do that? By planning your day trading strategies for the day and executing those strategies instead of just winging it.

As cliché as it may sound, failing to plan really is planning to fail. And considering the financial stakes involved in day trading, you shouldn't go through your trading days without any plan on hand. Luck favors those who are prepared and planning can convince lady luck that you are prepared.

Expecting Too Much Too Soon

This much is true about day trading: it's one of the most exciting and exhilarating jobs in the world! And stories many day traders tell of riches accumulated through this economic activity add more excitement, desire, and urgency for many to get into it.

However, too much excitement and desire resulting from many day trading success stories can be very detrimental to newbie day traders. Let me correct myself: it is detrimental to newbie day traders. Why?

Such stories, many of which are probably urban legends, give newbies unrealistic expectations of quick and easy day trading riches. Many beginner day traders get the impression that day trading is a get-rich-quick scheme!

It's not. What many day traders hardly brag about are the times they also lost money and how long it took them to master the craft enough to quit their jobs and do it full time. And even rarer are stories of the myriad number of people who've attempted day trading and failed. It's the dearth of such stories that tend to make day trading neophytes have unrealistic expectations about day trading.

What's the problem with lofty day trading expectations? Here's the problem: if you have very unrealistic expectations, it's almost certain that you'll fail. It's because unrealistic expectations can't be met and therefore, there's zero chances for success.

One of the most unrealistic expectations surrounding day trading is being able to double one's initial trading capital in a couple of months, at most. Similar to such expectations is that of being able to quit one's day job and live an abundant life in just a few months via day trading.

Successful day traders went through numerous failures, too, before they succeeded at day trading and were able to do it for a living.

Changing Strategies Frequently

Do you know how to ride a bike? If not, do you know someone who does? Whether it's you or somebody you know, learning how to ride a bike wasn't instant. It took time and a couple of falls and bruises along the way.

But despite falls, scratches and bruises, you or that person you know stuck to learning how to ride a bike and with enough time and practice, succeeded in doing so. It was because you or the other person knew that initial failures mean that riding a bike was impossible. It's just challenging at first.

It's the same with learning how to day trade profitably. You'll need to give yourself enough time and practice to master it. Just because you suffered trading losses in the beginning doesn't mean it's not working or it's not for you. It probably means you haven't really mastered it yet.

But if you quit and shift to a new trading strategy or plan quickly, you'll have to start again from scratch, extend your learning time, and possibly lose more money than you would've if you stuck around to your initial strategy long enough to give yourself a shot at day trading successfully or concluding with certainty that it's not working for you.

If you frequently change your day trading strategies, i.e., you don't give yourself enough time to learn day trading strategies, your chances of mastering them become much lower. In which case, your chances of succeeding in day trading becomes much lower, too.

Not Analyzing Past Trades

Those who don't learn history are doomed to repeat it, said writer and philosopher George Santayana. We can paraphrase it to apply to day traders, too: Those who don't learn from their day trading mistakes will be doomed to repeat them.

If you don't keep a day trading journal containing records of all your trades and more importantly, analyze them, you'll be doomed to repeat your losing day trades. It's because by not doing so, you won't be able to determine what you're doing wrong and what you should be doing instead in order to have more profitable day trades than losing ones.

Ditching Correlations

We can define correlations as a relationship where one thing influences the outcome or behavior of another. A positive correlation means that both tend to move in the same direction or exhibit similar behaviors, i.e., when one goes up, the other goes up, too, and vice versa.

Correlations abound in the stock market. For example, returns on the stock market are usually negatively correlated with the Federal Reserve's interest rates, i.e., when the Feds increase interest rates, returns on stock market investments go down and vice versa.

Correlations exist across industries in the stock market, too. For example, property development stocks are positively correlated to steel and cement manufacturing stocks. This is because when the property development's booming, it buys more steel and cement from manufacturing companies, which in turn also increase their income.

Ignoring correlations during day trading increase your risks for erroneous position taking and exiting. You may take a short position on a steel manufacturer's stock while taking a long position on a property development company's stock and if they have a positive correlation, one of those two positions will most likely end up in a loss.

But caution must be exercised with using correlations in your day trades. Don't establish correlations where there's none. Your job is to simply identify if there are observable correlations, what those correlations are, and how strong they are.

Being Greedy

Sadly for the owner, there were no golden eggs inside the goose because it only created and laid one golden egg every day. His greed caused him to destroy his only wealth-generating asset.

When it comes to day trading, greed can have the same negative financial impact. Greed can make a day trader hold on to an already profitable position longer than needed and result in smaller profits later on or worse, trading losses.

If you remember my story, that was greed in action. Had I been content with the very good returns I already had and closed my position, my paper gains could've become actual gains. I let my greed control my trading and chose to hold on to that stock much longer than I needed to. That trade turned into a losing one eventually.

That's why you must be disciplined enough to stick to your day trading stop-loss and profit-taking limits. And that's why you should program those limits on your platform, too. Doing so minimizes the risks of greed hijacking your otherwise profitable day trades.

Chapter 18 Trading Mindset And Psychology

To succeed in day trading, day traders require many skills, including the ability to analyze a technical chart. But none of the technical skills can replace the importance of a traders' mind-set. Discipline, quick thinking, and emotional control; all these are collectively called the trading psychology and are important factors for succeeding in the day trading business.

On the surface, day trading is an easy activity; markets go up and down and traders buy and sell with the price. Then how come 90% of traders make losses in day trading? The answer lies in trading psychology where most of the day traders fail. You will see many online courses advertising to teach day trading or technical analysis, but It is unheard of any course that teaching trading psychology to traders.

It is a well-known fact that controlling emotions of fear and greed are two of the most difficult decisions a day trader can take. Even those who prepare a trading plan, create trading rules; find it hard to stick to those rules and plans while trading in the stock markets. It is like dieting. When you are not supposed to think of ice cream, all you can do is think of ice cream.

Nobody is born with a successful trader's mindset. it is a skill developed with practice and self-discipline. Humans are emotional beings, so it is difficult to take emotions completely out of day trading. But traders can try to remain neutral and take the help of technology to trade, so their decisions are based on facts.

It is so easy to look at a chart and point, what was a good buying point and how much profit one could have made by trading in a certain way. But once markets open and the stock price starts changing its tracks, it sorts of hypnotizes traders in making wrong decisions. Emotions like greed and fear take over and traders keep making mistakes, accumulating losses instead of what should have been easy profits.

In stock markets, the simplest thing is the stock price's movement. It keeps going up or down rhythmically. Any child can tell when the price is going down, or when the price is going up. Still, day traders make the mistake of buying when the price is falling and selling when the price is rising. At any given time, half of the day traders believe that markets are at a good point to buy stocks, and the other half of day traders firmly believe that it is the right time to sell. Some of these traders are right half of the time, and some of these traders are wrong half of the time. Overall, none of them are right all the time. They get confused, not by the price movement; but by their own psychological reactions.

Understanding Trading Mindset and Psychology

For example, if a person is given two things to choose from, and given a time limit of 3 hours, he will do it in a relaxed way. However, if he is asked to decide within 3 seconds, he will panic. In other words, he will get into an emotional state.

Trading psychology involves two aspects; risk-taking and self-discipline. Traders know that emotions like greed and fear should not influence them, but they allow these emotions to affect their trading. Two other emotions are equally destructive; namely, hope and regret. Anger is an emotion that causes considerable loss to traders when they get frustrated by failure and indulge in revenge trading; which leads to more losses.

In greed, traders take more risk than is safe for them. In fear, traders avoid risk and generate very small profits.

Greed can encourage traders to indulge in over-trading. At times, it can cloud their rational thinking and judgment. It can lead to behavior that cannot be explained rationally. Traders may try to place big trades in a hurry to earn profits. If their trades are profitable, they may refuse to exit these trades even if the exit point has come and continue holding positions hoping for bigger profits. This behavior ultimately ends with loss because markets do not keep trending in one direction. Eventually, the market trend changes, and the profitable position turn into a loss-making one.

Fear has the opposite effect but the same result for traders. In the grip of fear, traders may close their position prematurely, then trade again to earn profits. It becomes a vicious cycle of fear and greed, where the trader is afraid to keep the position open longer but keeps trading again in greed.

Fear and Day Trading

The technical progress has made it possible for news to travel quick and reach far-flung places. This has created a unique situation for stock markets, where the positive news has a quick and positive reaction in the stock markets; but negative news causes sudden and a steep drop in stock prices as traders become gripped by fear and panic.

In situations leading to greed, traders still pause and think, if they are being greedy. But under the influence of fear, traders usually overreact and exit their position quickly. This has a chain-reaction effect on markets. Prices fall, traders sell in fear; prices fall further, traders sell more in fear. This emotion creates bigger ripples in stock markets than greed. Traders exit from their positions fearing that they will lose their profits or make losses. The fear of loss paralyzes novice traders when their positions turn into loss-making. They refuse to exit such positions, hoping for a bounce back in markets, hoping to turn their losses into profits. What should have been a small loss, eventually turns into a big one for them, sometimes even wiping out their all trading capital. A rationally thinking person will quickly exit from such a position. But fear is such strong emotion in day trading, that it stops even rational people from taking correct decisions.

Technology can help traders make the right decision in such situations. Automated trading is one aspect of trading that eliminates emotional content from day trading. But automated trading software is expensive and not every trader can afford those. Based on your trading plan, decide what will be your trade entry, exit, stop loss and profit booking levels.

To stop yourself from trading before the trade entry point has arrived, put a limit order for that level. It will free you from watching the price constantly. And, if you are not watching markets constantly, the chance of wrong trading is also removed.

You cannot remove emotions from life. Therefore, it will remain a part of your day trading business. But you can control it by self- discipline and proper trade management techniques. Patience is also one such technique, where you stay away from trading until the right trade entry level arrives.

Why Trading Psychology is Important

Most of the people fail in day trading because they start at the wrong end. They start by learning trading skills first, then move on to money and risk management techniques, and the last stop is to learn, superficially, about trading psychology.

In fact, the right sequence of learning day trading should be learning the trading psychology first, then money and risk management techniques and the last part should constitute learning the trading skills. It is very easy to learn technical analysis and how to use technical indicators. But it is very difficult to control one's emotions like fear and greed while trading, or astutely manage money while day trading.

If you look at people in different fields, you will find the mind-set is the main difference between those who reach the pinnacle of their chosen career and those who remain mediocre. Be it business, science, technology, sports, or any other creative pursuit, people who train their minds for success are the ones who win the race. In intraday trading also, hundreds and thousands of day traders use the same methods of technical analysis, however, only a few of them succeed in making profitable trade and others go home with losses. it is the trading psychology, that makes the difference between successful traders and those who failed.

Every trader, who tries to learn day trading, knows that there are certain rules to be followed and still the majority of them fail to do so find therefore if you want to succeed in day trading, you must pay attention to how you react to markets. stock trading is nothing but watching the price rise and fall and trading off with the trend. But still, traders fail to follow this simple method of trading. Day trading happens 90% in the mind of a day trader, and only 10% in what happens in markets. A day trader takes decision based on what he or she thinks is going to happen in stock markets, and not on what is happening. This is the biggest mistake of day traders do and the reason is their emotions.

To overcome this psychological hurdle, day traders must learn how to manage their trades without emotions. They can do so only with the help of technology, and self-discipline. If they do not have self-control or do not follow a disciplined trading plan, they cannot make profits in stock markets.

Chapter 19 Account Risk Management Entry Exit And Stop Loss

With any trade, risk management is an essential component despite the fact that it is often overlooked. It is crucial that day; traders learn about risk management if they are to successfully trade and remain profitable in the long term. The good news is that there are some simple strategies that can be adopted to ensure that trades are protected and risks management appropriately.

Basically, risk management is one of the most important aspects of the life of any serious day trader. The reason is that a trader can actually see 90% of their trades make money, but the 10% losing money may result in a net loss if there is no proper risk management. Therefore, it is important to plan all trades carefully and to take measures to protect all trades against any losses.

Trades should be Planned Appropriately

It is a well-known fact that a good strategy will win the war rather than the battle. A good day trader needs to plan and come up with a winning strategy as the first step. A lot of traders often live by the mantra, "Plan the trade and trade the plan." This is also very similar to war planning because those who plan properly are likely to win.

Take Profit and Stop Loss Points

Traders need to come up with two very important points. These points represent two major keys that enable traders to plan ahead or in advance. A good day trader ideally knows their entry point as well as their exit points. These important points will guide the trades and will indicate at what point the trader should buy stocks and at what point the stocks should be sold off.

When a trader determines the price they wish to pay for a stock and the price they wish to sell, then it is possible to find out the likelihood of the stock performing as desired. If this can be measured and confirmed, then the trader should enter and execute the trade.

Also, traders who enter a trade without making these kinds of determinations are likely to suffer loss and will in effect cease trading and instead gamble with his resources. Whenever traders start to make losses, they believe that they can always recover their money if they invest more. This is often a lack of discipline, and the trader is likely to lose even more money.

A stop-loss is defined as the actual price where a trader will choose to sell a stock and incur a loss on the particular trade. This is a situation that happens when trades do not proceed according to the trader's plans. These points are ideally designed in order to limit losses before they get out of hand. It is always tempting for a trader who is losing money to hang in there in the hope that the losing trend will end and profitability will resume once again.

Converse to this is the take-profit point. It is important to set the take-profit, which is really the price at which a trader exits a trade by selling the security and then takes a profit from the sale. The take point is often the point at which any additional upside will become limited beyond this point. Let us assume the trade approaches a key resistance level after a large upward movement then traders can choose to exit the trade at this point.

Improving the Risk Management Process

1. Setting the Risk: Reward Ratio

When an entry signal is sighted, work out the most appropriate place to locate the stop loss than first take the profit order. Now should the outcome not be satisfactory, then it is advisable to quit the trade. Traders should generally not attempt to reduce the stop loss or widen the profit order. Discipline, at this point, is very important.

Rewards in trade are never certain and are the only potential. It is the risk that traders have control over so it should be seriously considered. A lot of the time, inexperienced traders will take the opposite approach and later suffer the consequences.

2. Traders should Avoid Break-even Stops

Creating a no-risk trade by locating the stop loss close to the entry point is something that should be avoided at all costs. The reason is that this is a dangerous move and most often not profitable. While seeking some protection is advisable, these kinds of moves cause more harm than good and should always be avoided.

3. Fixed Stop Distances should not be used

Sometimes a trader may wish to make use of a fixed number of points on the stop loss then place profit orders on markets and varied instruments. These are essentially shortcuts and should not be used under any circumstances. The reason is that they often neglect price movements and the general operation of the markets.

Also, things such as momentum and volatility are never static but always changing depending on various factors. These will also have an effect on the price movement and will affect fluctuations over time. When volatility is high, profit order points and stop loss points need to be wider to maximize profits during price swings and to prevent any premature stop runs.

4. Risk-Reward and Win-Rate Ratios should be compared together

There are traders who do not believe in the win-rate ratio and consider it irrelevant. This is actually not a wise thought because it is a very important metric. Win-rate on its own is not a very useful metric, but when pitted against the risk vs. reward ratio, then it provides important insights.

Traders should Work Out their expected Returns

Traders need to be able to work out any expected returns from their trades. Now both take-profit and stop-loss points are essential to work out this figure. Expected returns provide an important figure that cannot be underestimated. This figure that results from the calculations causes a trader to think and rationalize their trades. It also ensures that only the most profitable trades are chosen.

How to Set the Stop-Loss Points

It is the technical analysis that mostly helps to determine the take-profit and stop-loss points. However, fundamental analysis of the stocks in question does play a crucial role, especially with the timing. For instance, if a trader is holding stock and the earnings report is around the corner, then such a trader will have to dispose of those shares before the news affects the markets. This is necessary regardless of whether the stock has hit the profit margin or not.

One of the most popular ways of setting up these points is to use the well-known Moving Average. Moving averages are pretty simple to work out and are tracked closely by market players. Some of the important Moving Averages include the 9, 20, 50, 100, and 200-day averages. These should typically be applied to any stock in question and then making a determination as to whether they have had an effect on its price or not.

Also, the support and resistance trend lines can be used to place the take-profit and stop-loss levels. First, the trader needs to draw these lines simply by connecting all the past lows or highs that appeared on the above average and significant volumes. The main aim here is to effectively determine the levels where the stock price is affected by the trend lines when volumes are significantly high.

Traders need to be able to determine at what points they enter and exit any traders that they wish to participate in. This determination needs to be made before the trade is actually entered. When indicators such as the stop-loss are effectively used, then the trader will be able to minimize their losses and also reduce the frequency with which trades are excited unnecessarily. The bottom line here is to prepare early, well ahead of time so as to be sure of success in all trades.

Chapter 20 Trading Business Plan

Aside from carefully evaluated day trading plans and strategies, here are other tips that can help optimize your day trading success.

Practice with a Trading Simulator First

These days, pilot trainees learn to fly airplanes on a simulator first before flying a real one. Why? By practicing with a flight simulator first, the risk of a pilot trainee crashing the plane becomes much lower. It's because flight simulators allow pilot trainees to experience how it is to fly a plane and how planes respond to controls without having to actually leave the ground. In case they commit major and potentially catastrophic mistakes during flight training, there will be no serious consequences other than low grades.

Day trading with real money on real stock or securities exchanges without first experiencing how it is to day trade is akin to learning how to fly a plane in a real plane in the sky! The risks of losing money are simply too high for a beginner to handle. By using your trading platform's trading simulator before day trading real money, you can afford to lose money as part of your learning process without actually losing money!

Stick to Your Daily Limits

While knowing how much capital you're willing to risk in day trading as a whole, you'll also need to have sub limits, i.e., daily limits. If you don't have such limits, it can be much easier to wipe out your entire trading capital in a day or two. A sensible guideline for your daily limit is to cut your losses when your daily trading position registers a maximum loss of 10%.

Avoid Becoming Attached to Your Stocks

As a newbie trader, your chances of becoming emotionally attached to your chosen SIPs are high. That's why a big chunk of the trading strategies enumerated earlier involve using numbers as triggers for entering and exiting positions in SIPs. Numbers are objective and if you stick to them, you can prevent your emotions from hijacking your trades.

Feel the Mood of the Market

Technical analysis, via candlestick charts and technical indicators, are very good ways to gauge the market's mood. However, they're not perfect and you may need to validate their readings by interacting with actual traders.

Trade Patiently

Only fools rush in, as the saying goes. However, it can be very easy to rush into trades, especially for newbies, when a significant amount of time has passed without any trades. It's because it can seem that one is wasting time by not trading.

The truth is, time will be wasted, as well as trading capital, by rushing into trades for the sake of making them. Remember, the point of day trading is to make money and not to simply trade. If no good opportunities are available, there's no need to force a day trade. Be patient and wait for trading signals to appear before taking positions.

Befriend Your Losing Trades

Nobody's perfect. That includes day traders. Even the very best still get into losing day trades, albeit their total trading profits significantly exceed their total trading losses.

Knowing that even the best of the best still have their share of losing trades should make you feel much better about losing trades. Even better, why not look at them from a different perspective just like how Thomas Edison looked at his "failed" experiments.

When asked about the first 1,000 failed experiments on the working light bulb, Edison corrected his interviewer by saying those weren't failed experiments. They were successful experiments because each of those first 1,000 light bulb experiments showed him how not to make the light bulb and in so doing, brought him a step closer to making a working version of the bulb.

Choose Your Broker Wisely

Many newbie day traders choose their brokers without really giving it much thought. Probably it's because they're overwhelmed with so many new things to learn that they fail to pay attention to the brokers they choose. Don't make the same mistake because remember, you'll be entrusting your precious day trading capital, which in the United States is a minimum of $25,000. And that's a lot of money to entrust, which means choosing a trustworthy and excellent day trading broker is a must.

With so many new online brokers popping up on the Internet these days, it can be quite challenging to sift through the reputable and not-so-reputable ones. Fortunately, there are many online resources and forums on which you can glean information on online brokers' reputations and quality of service.

Part of choosing the right broker is platform or order execution speed. Remember, day trading success is very dependent on how fast you can execute your orders in the market. So, choose a broker that's not just reputable but has a fast order-executing platform.

Don't Scrimp on Technology

I can't emphasize enough the importance of speed when it comes to day trading, where a mere few seconds can spell the difference between profitable and losing trades. For this, you can't afford to settle for the cheapest hardware and software, which most likely be too slow for consistent day trading success.

Now, I'm not saying you should get the most expensive, top-of-the-line computers for your day trading activities. It'll be like trying to kill a fly with a shotgun. However, your primary consideration for buying a computer and choosing an Internet service providers should be technical specifications. Price should only be the secondary factor and fortunately, you don't need to buy an iMac or a MacBook Pro just to day trade with sufficient speed.

Also, make sure that you have either a landline or a cellular phone line to reach your broker in the event that your Internet connection acts up for one reason or another. Better to err on the side of caution than on the side of negligence, don't you think?

Focus on Price Movements and News Triggers or Catalysts

Day trading relies on technical analysis and very little on fundamental analysis, except for news catalysts or triggers. And by nature of its reliance on technical analysis, it doesn't bother itself with a company's financial data and the like.

Why am I reminding you of this? One way you can sabotage your day trading success is by overanalyzing your stocks or securities. When you extend your research and analysis on a company's balance sheet and income statement items, as well as industry and economic trends, you'll spend too much time on things that aren't really important to day trading. Fundamental analysis is crucial for swing trading and long-term investing but with day trading, all you need to focus on is price movement and significant news announcements.

Stick to those two only so you can make the most out of your day trading time and so that you can enter and exit positions on a timely basis.

Conclusion

T hank you for making it through to the end of Day Trading, let's hope it was educative and able to provide you with all of the tools you need to achieve your goals whatever they may be.

You may have in mind the market that would interest you to trade. You should be in a position to find a repeating pattern that would be quite convenient to exploit and make profits from. As earlier indicated, no market is better than the other. What differentiates it is your capital investment and what exactly you want to trade. You realize that some markets may vary depending on the time of operation, e.g., for forex, it runs 24/7. In others, they do not charge any commissions. Other markets have high volatility; hence, the traders enjoy huge trade swings. This may work both as an advantage or a disadvantage since theses swing also mean enormous risks of huge losses. Do not take the risk to try to master all the markets that come your way. You just need to focus on one so as to avoid having divided attention. The moment you learn to make profits from one of the markets, it becomes easier to master the rest. If the wins are many and give high returns, then setting your stop loss a bit high would only work better for you as that would translate to higher profits. The idea of managing your risks is to make your losses quite small such that one single day of winning can compensate for the accrued losses.

The next step is to get started with some of the work that we are able to do when it comes to day trading. There are a lot of investment styles that are out there, and some of them are going to be simple to work with, and some are a bit harder to handle along the way. Being able to put them together and learn how to utilize day trading and the fast world that it belongs to could be the key that you need to see a lot of success.

This guidebook took some time to talk and explore all of the different parts that we need to know when it comes to day trading. There are a lot of people who are skeptical about working with day trading because they think it will fail at it, or they think that it is too risky. But with some of the methods and strategies that we have talked about in this guidebook ready to go, even someone who has not had a chance to do any investing at all in the past will be able to see some results.

CPSIA information can be obtained
at www.ICGtesting.com
Printed in the USA
LVHW080536261020
669798LV00006B/258

9 781801 116602